A Room Nearby

Daniel & Kathy Baker

GHOSTRYDER PRESS

Published by Ghostryder Press

ISBN-13: 978-0-9833891-0-1
Library of Congress Control Number: 2011923496

Book design by Brion Sausser (www.bookcreatives.com)
Printed in the United States of America

Dedication

In Loving Memory of My Father, Leonard Doss
May 8th, 1929-July 12, 2010
Until we meet again in A Room Nearby

Acknowledgments

To my God, the creator of all things, for allowing me the opportunity to learn those lessons needed to evolve and to once again return to His side in our heavenly home-I prayed and He heard.

For my daughters Katrina and Kimberly, there are no words I can say to express my deepest love and gratitude. You have filled my life with so much joy, laughter, and love. How blessed I have been to know you both.

To my husband Dan who has been my best friend, my lover, and most certainly my soul-mate. You stood by me faithfully thru all the ups and downs and never doubted me. Your passion has been felt on every page of this book. I am certain we will spend eternity together.

I also wish to thank my brother Rob and my sister Cynthia for re-entering my life at a time when I most needed you. May the bonds that tie be never broken.

To my mother whom I have always loved and who I now know has always loved me, thank you for difference you have made in my life.

And to my father, may we meet again under different circumstances with a newfound respect and love for one another.

Contents

Foreword

In May of 1985 while giving birth to my first child, I died. I flat lined for a full eight minutes. During those minutes I underwent a Death Experience. I call what happened to me a Death Experience as opposed to the more commonly used phrase "Near Death Experience", simply because I was fully dead during this ordeal.

Most Death Experiences as recounted by various people tend to describe the same types of experiences with perhaps only minor differences. They differ in ways that our life experiences differ from person to person.

While my personal Death Experience operated within the accepted framework of what we have all come to know as your basic Near Death Experience, it differed in a number of ways and answered many questions left unanswered.

Many of the miracles that I was witness to conflicted at times with contemporary religious belief, but all too often it also agreed with and confirmed the truth of Biblical teachings.

Since mankind has had a hand in writing and re-writing history it is my belief that somewhere along the way basic truths became slightly muddled. Clarity must be achieved and at times the ability to clearly see presents itself in ways we could never have imagined.

The high spiritual crime of suicide is a case in point. While on the other side I met with my Grandmother who I had never known in this lifetime. I learned from her that before I was born she had taken her own life. It became evident while speaking to her that we had known each other throughout the ages and while in many earthly guises.

It was through this encounter that I came to understand that the act of suicide was indeed one of the worse possible acts that one could commit, but not for those reasons generally believed and accepted.

When we come into this life we metaphorically enter into a contract. Before each new incarnation we enter, we leave that world and enter this one with many grand expectations and much enthusiasm with high hopes of succeeding and weathering through those lessons and obstacles that are placed before us.

Failure to achieve these spiritual ends is not an option nor is it even considered.

But then we emerge into the physical-a condition that is truly foreign to the Soul. We find ourselves in a dense and confining environment, limited by physical laws. We have chosen the most harsh and punishing of learning centers for the purposes of spiritual growth. The Angels themselves hail our bravery and fortitude as they urge us onwards.

Unfortunately many souls falter during this process!

After contracting an anomalous jungle disease while working as a Nurse, I too contemplated suicide. It is truly a terrible state of mind to be in. After nearly three years of being bed ridden and suffering terrible agonies and debilities I had enough. The medical profession informed me it was only a matter of time before I died and I was told to make peace with my God. But it was because of the grace of God that I maintained my sanity and clung to life-it is what brought me through.

Many who take their own lives find themselves in a hell like state. It is estimated that fully 10% of those who return from a Death Experience tell of terrible punishments on "the other side". Some describe scenes reminiscent of Dante's Inferno, while others remark that they found themselves surrounded by darkness and despair. What they all tend to agree on is that once they cried out for help, they were taken out of their hellish predicament only to experience a heaven like setting or, they are returned to their physical body with a renewed vigor to live life in a positive and loving way.

In the case of my Grandmother, the hell that she created for herself was the decision to stay on the Earth Plane, for fear of retribution, refusing to enter "the light", becoming what we commonly refer to as a Ghost!

It was only after pleading for help that help was given and she was taken back to her heavenly home. Her greatest remorse was that she made the wrong decision in ending her earthly life. She finally understood that the life she took failed to end the misery she was suffering. She came to understand that she had "broken the contract" and would have to face the same set of circumstances once again in a future life. What she experienced in life were those lessons chosen by her higher self for the benefit of soul growth. My Grandmother realized that even the most miserable day on Earth is a blessing and a valuable gift not to be wasted.

We are never given more than we can handle. No matter how bad things appear in the present we can over come them with prayer. We need only suffer through and endure them because the lessons they deliver are more precious than we know.

The Aborigines of Australia believe that when we are awake, we are dreaming, and when we are asleep, that sleep time is our reality.

Who are we to dispute this claim?

I have been shown that what we assume as "Reality" is created by consciousness and thought at all levels of life and originates at the God head, then merges into the collective consciousness of all living entities. What we take for granted as "Reality" is quite simply a set of laws borne from the collective beliefs of mankind called Consensus. The effects of physical laws in which we operate are not fixed but may shift according to the state of collective consciousness. Although a very persistent illusion, physical reality remains just that-an illusion. Reality is but a concentration of collective thought and belief projected onto a holographic universe and becomes our "reality". Although it lends the appearance of being fixed, it is nevertheless always in a state of flux and is malleable by agreement.

The basic rules of physics were brought about by consensus reality, but it was in accordance with the Grand Masters plan as a way to learn those many spiritual lessons when interacting with one another. These interactions are limited and controlled through governing constraints and parameters of action for the benefit of all participants.

Reality is what we have made it! We have all co-created with the Master of the Universe.

In *A Room Nearby* I endeavor to explain the totality of my experience and attempt to sift through what is important and what is but mere window dressing and distractions in the drama we call life.

I also wanted to describe in detail my many experiences with "other worldly beings" and how these phenomena are intimately tied to our reality on the earth plane. I cannot definitively explain the origins of these hauntings as I believe most of these entities spring from multi-faceted realities and bring with them various intentions and motivations. I cannot disallow nor exclude this part of the puzzle from my writing because to do so would only marginalize the overall message.

I began this book almost ten years ago and many family members urged me on to complete it. Some became quite frustrated in the fact that it was taking so long. I must admit that I was at a loss to explain the seemingly endless delays in its completion.

I felt as though there was a guiding hand helping me in the writings, and this guiding force was also responsible in choosing the time of its completion, but for what reason?

The realization occurred to me that the delay involved the necessary completion of a cycle. There was an ending that was not quite complete. I didn't understand for a long time what that ending might be or, if indeed there was one at all.

In early childhood I became the victim of mental and physical abuse by the man who I loved and I believed loved me-my father. The torment would last for many years and the abuse would have a profound affect on me and would change the course of my life in its entirety.

In a family with four children, my father choose me as the focal point of his rage, frustration, and violent attacks.

I have come to understand and believe that I was placed before my father as an example to him of what is possible when love is expressed and subsequently embraced unconditionally.

Many who know of my early life have remarked that they are astounded that I never turned to drugs or prostitution, or became an abuser of my own children, or in some other way found a means of self-destruction. To them I can only say that I believe I was chosen for the position within the family because I was in fact a "safe" choice. By safe I mean I would not allow a less developed soul, a newer soul shall we say, the opportunity to de-evolve that part of me that took a millennia to achieve. In affect I was safe from a reversion to a lower state. I was the perfect subject and guide for my father's evolvement.

I would not allow the insanity to continue by inflicting the same sort of punishment on my own children nor anyone else close to me. In affect I had broken the chain my father attempted to weave.

Of the many conclusions I have arrived at, I believe that the relationship I had with my father was the most important aspect of this lifetime. It is why I choose to be here.

My father has recently left this world and returned to his true home, one filled with unconditional love and light. With his departure I was given the authority to complete these writings.

I can only pray that from somewhere up above he is looking down approvingly in the knowledge that our story has finally been told.

CHAPTER ONE

Transition

I have been in labor now for nineteen hours. How can I possibly endure this any longer? Only a woman could handle the pain of this process. My Mother described in graphic detail the pangs and torment she suffered explaining it was the hardest of all things to bear. She proudly added that it was also the easiest to forget. "Easy to forget. How could anyone forget this?" I thought. But for the moment at least the labor continued and I had no idea how much longer it would last. Nature wasn't allowing me to rest as the contractions came at an increasingly faster pace.

They refer to this process as the miracle of childbirth. Little did I know then that I was about to experience multiple miracles.

Childbirth is a miracle of this realm but it also involves an intermixing of multi-dimensional miracles. I would be a witness to these miracles and more. I would be allowed to glimpse secrets that are reserved only for those who have graduated to the other side.

There is magic we call nature that in all her glory can at times orchestrate unimaginable pain. The pain is followed by a bit of release or calming only to repeat itself in a seemingly endless cycle. The rhythm of nature is precise in her timing and unrelenting as the crescendo of birth is actualized.

Suddenly the pain was gone. I could breathe again. "I must gather my thoughts," I told myself. I understood that pain was merely the constriction of consciousness and that a state of bliss is an expansion of this consciousness. The greater the expansion of mind the more extreme the state of bliss. Fully understanding this I needed to develop a plan. "This is simple," I thought. During the next contraction I would simply 'expand' my consciousness thereby relieving or reducing the pain.

I was good at this. I was practiced. After all I believed I had the keys to all understanding! Reality was what I made of it. I was well versed in the study of Eastern Religion and the esoteric. I was also highly intuitive since birth. I had the edge. I knew what I was doing.

Or so I thought.

Right on time Mother Nature struck again. I braced for its impact by focusing on the universe, on my third eye and on the light.

It didn't work.

I screamed in disgust. A wave of unutterable pain swept through my body. I felt I was going to levitate off of the bed. I screamed at the top of my lungs to anyone in the room who could hear.

The scene must have been quite comical. Mark, my husband whom I have been married to for 18 months was the only one present in the hospital room and I doubt that those utterances had any impact on him. It didn't matter. I had made my point. "Let's try it again. Breathe in deep, release, breath again. It can't be that bad can it?" said Mark in a calm unaffected tone. I was desperate. I would try anything because the breathing routine just wasn't working.

I read once that one indicator of insanity was repeating something over and over in a vain attempt to make it work, but despite knowing its futility you continue to repeat it. Once again I braced for the pain that I knew was coming. I felt I was going insane and perhaps to a certain degree I was.

Just then my Doctor entered the room. Leaning over the bed he looked into my eyes and said "Kathy as you know we have induced delivery since you haven't dilated enough. We will be taking you in for an emergency Cesarean." With those words many emotions began to fill my mind. I had hoped for a natural delivery, but more importantly I wanted a healthy baby. I felt and I knew that the baby would be healthy. I also felt a sense of foreboding that I couldn't quite put my finger on. Something began to nag at me and it was as sudden and as overwhelming as the contractions that had once again begun only moments ago.

A few minutes passed when two of the labor and delivery Nurses entered my room and began to take my vitals and shave all necessary areas. Mark who was seated across the room continued his helpless stare periodically checking his watch. Why the time checks I wondered. I glanced toward the wall clock. "Nothing new there." I thought.

The contractions continued and the pain was even more intense. Once again I screamed out aloud and was promptly told by one of the attending nurses to "Shut up!"

I looked toward Mark who was once again checking his watch. "Why do you keep checking the time?" I howled. Mark looked at me with a blank expression. I then turned to the nurse who told me to shut up praying she had something else to say. She was silent except for the very loud grin she was wearing. I despised her callousness. I despised Mark. I despised the world.

Fatigue and pain wracked my body and mind. I was placed on a gurney and wheeled toward the operating room. My sight was blurred and I grimaced as I starred at the succession of lights on the ceiling as I glided noiselessly through the hallway. In the distance I could hear laughter. "How could they laugh at a time like this?" I thought. The smell of antiseptics filled my nostrils. These were familiar sights and sounds to me. After all I worked at this Hospital. In fact I would be assigned to this floor quite routinely as an LVN. Now of course I was seeing it from the perspective of a patient.

Professionally I regarded all patients with a detached objectivity. I now wondered how this experience might change me. If nothing else it was humbling. How dare that nurse tell me to shut up? Where was her empathy?

Mark continued to hold my hand until being ordered to move away by the Doctor. The operating team lifted me onto the operating table. Organized confusion seemed to rule the moment as doctors and nurses readied the room. My vision was still blurred and I had to squint to focus. Fast moving arms and bodies distorted the intensely bright lights that flooded my watery eyes. I reassured myself that this was a routine procedure. After all I professionally knew all three Doctors present in the room.

The operating room staff was still awaiting the arrival of the fourth Doctor, the Anesthesiologist who had just been called in to assist in the delivery.

Finally after what seemed like hours the doors to the operating room flew open and in walked one of the doctors who appeared infuriated; "Why the hell was I the one to be called out on this one?" No one answered. He was in a controlled rage. I strained to focus on him. Apart from knowing this Doctor professionally I also considered him a friend. I knew his wife. Everyone is aware that he and his wife were in the midst of a very nasty divorce. Rumors and gossip flooded the halls and coffee rooms of the hospital concerning these two. I must admit that I too was not immune to its intoxicating allure as I was considered by staff to be somewhat of an authority on the subject. I'm not sure why, but if anyone wanted to know anything they always came to me for the secrets.

I don't think the Doctor prior to entering the operating room knew that I was his patient. Perhaps he did, but didn't care. Perhaps things would have ended differently if he knew it was I.

As I continued to focus on him, I felt an overwhelming sense of pain and frustration that seemed to spill from his very being. A feeling of desperation filled me. That feeling of desperation then turned to one of panic. I had to control myself. I was barely able to utter a "hello" as the next wave of contractions began to rush in. Doctors and staff completed the final preparations as I continued to writhe in pain. One of the Doctors informed me that they were about to administer the epidural.

"Finally, my suffering was to come to an end," I thought. I said a silent prayer.

More than anything else, I wanted to hold my newly born child in my arms. I exhaled closing my eyes I resigned myself to the joy that was sure to follow. My mind darted through time and I imagined an intensely wonderful relationship with my new daughter as I guided her through life. She would fulfill me and I would be the best mother imaginable. I was about to enter a new life one filled with a perfect love that only a Mother and Child could create.

The Anesthesiologist having learned whom his new patient was leaned over and gently began to raise me up. "Kathy," he said, "let's sit up now. I am going to insert the catheter." I gradually rose into a fetal position on the table. It was a cumbersome struggle to attain this position since the baby was full term and the last contraction had no yet subsided. I struggled into position because I trusted the Doctor, but I was still a bit concerned about his mental state. He had calmed himself dramatically and for this I was relieved.

As a Nurse I was well aware that epidurals were very risky procedures. If the needle slipped or was placed improperly death could quickly result. The Epidural Block Procedure is known to have a one in eight hundred thousand probability of terminal failure. "What were the chances," I thought. "I had a better chance winning the Lottery than experiencing a problem with the procedure!"

Gradually I felt the needle being placed into my back. Moments later I was slowly lowered back into a prone position. I once again closed my eyes and breathed deeply.

As I lay observing the blackness of my consciousness, swirls and pinpoints of light danced and darted about in random fashion. To my amazement the randomness began to disappear and slowly form in the center of my mental screen to what appeared to be the outline of a person. Slowly the form took shape. In black and white I was able to discern the shape of a person from just below the shoulders to the top of his head. As this shape crystallized I felt I was observing someone familiar to me. "Perhaps this was my guardian angel or Guide or even a relative who had gone to the other side and who is now here to help me through my ordeal," I thought. "But wait," I thought again to myself. The feeling that was radiating from this being wasn't good. He was menacing. I focused on this entity. I looked him directly in the eyes and he looked back. I braced myself as my breathing patterns became faster and deeper.

The specter that I beheld was that of an old man. Gaunt and with deep lines accenting his face he had a large bird like nose and thin unsmiling lips. His stare was penetrating and unyielding. He was grizzled and unshaven. On his head he wore a large brimmed hat, dark and wrinkled it sat low on his head. He was obviously not of this era.

Almost imperceptibly I became aware of a numbing in my midsection. I found that my breathing had become shallow and labored. The image of the old man began to fade.

The next thing I knew I found myself gasping for air. I tried to inhale but it was futile - my lungs were unable to expand. The doctor behind me leaned over and, with his face only inches from mine, asked, "Kathy, what's the matter?" The panicked look in his eyes said much more than his veiled question. With what must have been the last bit of remaining air in my lungs, and almost inaudibly I said my last words.

"I'm dying."

My lungs suddenly stopped working completely. I was unable to take another breath and uncontrollable waves of sheer panic over took me. Almost simultaneously both of my wrists were wrenched tightly and strapped down. An oxygen mask was placed over my face. I began to violently convulse. I remember thinking that this is what it felt like to die.

In the twinkling of the eye I found myself floating near the ceiling. There was no warning, no noise, and no lifting out of body. I was simply "there." I focused my attention downward and understood that I was observing an operation involving me. I continued to stare at the operating team who appeared to be in a very excited state. I distinctly remember hearing "Her heart has stopped!"

Incredibly, I remember thinking, "Lucky me! One in eight hundred thousand and it had to be me!"

In the middle of this madness I was able to discern my physical body. From the solar plexus region ran a brilliantly lit silvery cord that undulated slightly from side to side almost as if it had a life of its own. It ran straight up from my body and disappeared within the other "me."

As I continued to watch the scene below I became aware of other silvery brightly lit strands projecting outwards from the doctors and nurses. There were so many and they were running in so many directions. It reminded me of a spider's web. These strands interconnected from person to person. They were not as large as the one running from my physical body to my other body but almost thread-like in size. They appeared to be of the same color and intensity of the cord that attached me to the physical realm. These strands coursed from one person and would connect with everyone in the room. Each person repeated this to the other.

I saw a nurse hurriedly enter the room from the hallway and instantaneously the energy strands struck her from every person in the room. She in turn projected to everyone else in the room. It was all instantaneous.

A profound truth overtook me. Like everyone else I have heard that we are all connected to each other. Up to this point I considered it a nice thought and a possibility that probably involved our thought processes somehow linking us magically to each other.

This I now know beyond a shadow of doubt and will share with you. It concerns the connecting energies of life.

There is an existence nearby. It is very different from the one you are experiencing now. In fact there are many existences. It is not a place that exists in the clouds and it does not exist somewhere in space. It presses upon you, it envelops you, it caresses you and begs to be touched and explored by you. It is right next to you! At times it gives glimpses of itself in many different ways. It is the many "houses" that you have read of. Your passport to these

realms is ready. You merely need to change your vibratory reso-
nance. When you go there you actually go nowhere. You simply
switch. You are still right here. And in this place there is no time.

Albert Einstein once said; "Time and Space are modes by
which we think, not conditions in which we live" Albert never
knew just how correct he was.

As I continued to view these amazing dancing threads it occurred to me that even within this plane or realm there are governing laws - laws of physics if you will. They are as fixed and
unyielding as those on the earthly plane. They encompass all truth.
You need only change your vibratory state to enter this alternate
level.

The "connecting threads of energy" are a part of this reality. It
doesn't matter that you can't see these threads while in the bodily
plane for I can assure you they exist. We are not only connected to
each other but we also connect to all living things including plant
life and minerals.

When I was a little girl from time to time the theatres would
feature 3-D movies that issued special glasses at the door. When
the glasses are used at the beginning of the show the normally 2-D
Movies that we were used to were now viewable in 3-D. The entire
perception of the movie was greatly enhanced by the frames. It
was mesmerizing and almost impossible to put into words and to
describe to someone who had never been to a 3-D viewing.

It was the same in that state. Everything was greatly defined.
The outlines of the operating crew were more distinct, clearer, and
more animated. Colors took on a different hue and texture. It was

an immersion into the environment. I felt I could almost hear the colors and taste them. They seemed to speak to me.

Sound too took on a different reality. Though I could clearly hear the conversations taking place below me it seemed somehow muffled or lost in the additional tones and vibrations emanating from everything. The walls, floors, and ceiling seemed to projecting their own tones and sounds. I remember focusing on the upper metal portion of the light fixture just above the operating table where my lifeless body now lay. As I momentarily fixed my gaze on the light I began to perceive a distinct tone or vibration that seemed to be coming from the light fixture itself. Each and every "expression" on this plane has its own vibratory "signature"

I floated in complete awe and disbelief. Truly I was in a different world, but I was still observing a reality I was fully immersed in just a few moments ago. I can only describe the delight that I experienced at that moment as child-like. It was like the feeling you had as a very young child as you discovered this new world you were in, this earthly plane with its new delights and surprises seemingly everywhere.

As we grow older we lose this feeling and some of us may find no intrigue or wonder left. Perhaps this feeling is lost simply to the repetitiveness of our existence. I believe that as a young child you are not quite "fazed in" to this dimension. You are actually somewhere between this one and the one you just left and it may take quite a few years before you are completely "fazed out" of the dimension you left only a few years before. Once this occurs fully there is a quelling of the immense joy that followed you here. You become more attuned and set into this dimension. Everything becomes narrowed and restricted. Therefore much of the joy is lost.

The symphony of sound overcame me as I continued to drift and float above the life and death drama unfolding below me. As I watched I felt myself becoming more and more detached from its apparent importance.

"Why do they rush around so frantically?" I thought. "I am fine," I cry out but no one hears me. "I'm alright, leave me alone. She's okay!" "Are they deaf," I wondered?

It then occurred to me once again that I was having a baby and what was to become of the Baby if they could not revive me? To be perfectly honest I didn't care. I knew the Baby would be all right. I was not of this world any longer. What seemed real moments ago no longer seemed real. What was important just moments ago were no longer important. I was free of my body and I was free of the confines of Earthly conceptions. I was free of the illusion.

Suddenly and coming somewhere from my left I heard a male voice say to me "Don't be afraid, just go along with it." I looked around and saw a radiant being. I couldn't make out his features: no face, no clothing, only the brilliantly lit outline of His presence.

As I continued to stare at this being whose radiance would have blinded me had I been in the physical I felt an urge to look behind me. I cannot say that I turned my head to look. It was more of a redirecting of my consciousness that allowed me to look behind myself.

As I "turned" I found that the ceiling behind me had disappeared. In its place was a swirling vortex, tornado like, snaking, undulating, alive, and reaching to the heavens. Various thoughts danced through my mind as I attempted to comprehend the enormity of what I was seeing. I thought of Jack and the Beanstalk. I wondered how I was supposed to climb this towering behemoth and what would I find at the end. I chuckled at the very thought.

As the vortex slowly revolved and twisted it positioned itself above me so that I was able to see its rounded interior walls. Its length seemed almost endless and appeared to pierce the depths of the universe.

I moved ever so slightly positioning myself for a better look. I could see clearly now. The light at the top was so intense that it reminded me of a welder's light that I had once seen at a car repair shop as a little girl. This light appeared to ever so slightly illuminate the rounded wall of the vortex and extended its entire length. The walls were soft and billowy looking. The light at the top lent a grayish brown hue to the illuminated insides of the tunnel.

The light at the top appeared to intensify. It engulfed me. It gently called out to me. It was the light of heaven. This I knew. I knew I must go up. My only question was who would be waiting for me if once I reached the top.

As I continued to look, the same voice, but now behind me, urged me onward. "Kathy, do not be afraid to go to the light." I froze. The gigantic swirling tornado like mass was continuing its slow rotation. Suddenly a wave of what can only be described as total love and acceptance rushed through me. I knew that it had come from the same being who was urging me forward.

All fear and lingering ambivalence drained from my being as if the gates to my soul had been opened and all negative and restrictive emotion had finally been set free. To my delight my whole being began to vibrate. The vibration rose in frequency, subtle at first, but then growing in intensity until I felt I was going to burst with the force of an exploding star.

In an instant I was projected upwards. It was like being shot out of a cannon. Faster and faster I rose and I felt myself being propelled at the speed of light. Strangely enough I also felt like I was being flattened. I was being pulled not pushed.

I watched as I quickly passed by the sides of the tunnel. I focused my gaze upwards and began to see small specks of light interspersed around the tunnel. As I rose these specks of light became larger. I quickly passed the first one and was able to see that the light was in the shape of a person. The being was glimmering in all the colors of the rainbow. He seemed to be pressed into the wall of the tunnel as if he were part of it. As I shot upwards I was once again struck with waves of love and compassion that radiated from this light being who was now disappearing below me.

Higher and higher I rose. To my right was another beautifully glimmering light being. Once again I was overcome with peace and love. I passed countless beings of light during my ascent. It was becoming addictive. I could have spent the rest of my existence in this tunnel.

As I ascended and came closer to the light I became aware that the sides of the tunnel began to slowly constrict in width. I also became aware of music. It was like symphony music. The music I heard however was far beyond tunes that any mortal being can muster with an instrument. It was the orchestrations of heaven and it was emanating from the light at the end of the tunnel.

As I reached the top I heard a loud "whooshing" noise and in the next instant I found myself standing before what I can only describe as a throne. The centerpiece of this throne was an immense chair made of gold. Behind the chair and in all directions was the vastness of space and all of the objects contained in space. I could see distant stars, galaxies, and comets racing through space.

Suspended above the golden chair was a glorious round pulsating light. The light shone of every color imaginable. It pulsated as though breathing. The intensity of the light was blinding. Having no physical eyes to see with I still felt a need to turn away from its brilliance. I looked back and found that I was able to continue looking without turning again.

I thought that I must be face to face with God. I was enveloped in its presence and felt that I had become one with the universe. The intimacy I felt with this spirit is unspeakable.

A voice spoke to me. The voice was neither male nor female, but androgynous in its tone. "You are not ready to stay here, soon you must go back. You will be shown many things but you will not remember them all, as you will be incapable of retaining most these ideas when you go back into the world. Trust in me and trust in yourself for you have always been mine. But first you must see what was and what is destined to be."

Instantly the scene before me disappeared and I beheld the Earth below me as if I was watching it from outer space. I could see the oceans and the continents with colors so vibrant and clear.

I could even see cloud covers and lightning strikes on different lands.

I became aware that I was also surrounded by thousands of others. Looking around me I saw people who I knew and those who I didn't. We were in a pastoral setting with green rolling hills and ponds spaced here and there.

Some of those who I was now with were sitting while others were standing. There was great anticipation in what was about to take place. In the distance I saw Cats and Dogs running through the pastures. I looked back around and once again the Earth came into view.

Then I realized that I was among those who were waiting to be reborn again. Those who stood and sat nearby were waiting for the exact moment when they would be ushered into their new existence on the Earthly plane. The area that we were in was the launching pad to this new life.

I understood even before my death that reincarnation was a truth. You experienced many life times. When you died you entered an area somewhere between the Earthly Plane and a plane referred to in western religions as heaven. During this period of rest you evaluated your past life, continued to learn in this new realm, and prepared for your next incarnation.

So what was I doing here among those whose departure back to Earth was imminent?

Everyone was jubilant. I felt as though I was waiting to board a cruise ship for a trip around the world. I also wondered how these souls could be so happy to incarnate back into an existence full of so much pain and sorrow. After all I had just left there and the memories were fresh in my mind. "Had they so soon forgotten the sufferings of this Earthly dimension?" Why were they so eager to return?

CHAPTER TWO

A Review

As I pondered this question I slowly looked around in utter awe at the beauty before me. Suddenly I felt a hand on my shoulder. Startled I looked around and saw before me a young woman who was perhaps in her late twenties, vibrant and glowing. Her hair was brown and she had green eyes that pierced my heart. She wore a white lightweight one-piece dress that was tied with a bow below her neck. The dress around the waist was also tied off in a bow. She smiled at me and looked as though she was ready to burst with excitement. "I am your Grandmother Kathryn", she said as she threw both her arms up and out. I stepped backwards in disbelief. She stepped toward me and took me into both her arms and hugged me tightly.

She was stunning in her beauty, but I still did not recognize her. "Who are you?" I stammered.

"I am your Grandmother Kathryn and although we have never met I know all about you! I am here to answer all your questions. I have waited a great while to meet you my Darling"

It had been almost forty years since she "died". I had only recently been told of some of the circumstances surrounding her death. My Mother was reticent in telling me anything concerning my Grandmother other than that she was born in Russia and together they immigrated to Shanghai during WWII. I also knew that while in Shanghai my Mother met and married my Father Leonard.

My Grandmother immigrated to the USA in 1951. She arrived in San Francisco, California. Alone and penniless she settled there. The very last of her money was spent on the rental of an apartment in the Mission District of that strange and fabulous City.

On December 1951 at the age of 50 she hung herself in her apartment. Her Death Certificate indicated that at the time of Death she was unemployed. They did not find her for three days. She had committed one of the cardinal sins of western religion having taken her own life.

This was the depth of my knowledge concerning my Grandmother.

"Grandma, what-" She stopped me in mid-sentence and said "I will tell you of my experience, what happened to me in the 'between state' and what was to follow, how I arrived here, and what I must do next."

She was obviously very excited to tell me the story of her life. She once again turned her gaze toward me and almost shook with excitement.

"My darling Kathryn you are not aware of my entire life. I know that you were not told much of the sufferings that I endured and the mistakes I made. Why your mom and dad kept it all a secret I will never know. I am going to tell you of these things and much more. I know that you will understand and forgive me for I have forgiven myself, and self-forgiveness is the most important thing. You will see that these things are true. It is a part of your education."

Her gaze turned from me and toward the Earth below as she began her story. As she spoke images flashed before my mind in quick sequence. I could not only hear her, but I could also visualize, in panoramic detail, those things of which she spoke as though she placed the images into my mind.

"Kathryn", she began, "Life in Russia was, for our entire family, one of toil, shortages, hunger, despair, and war. I was born at the turn of the Century in a land that for you would be hard to imagine. Most of the time I went to bed hungry, but the love of my Mother and Father more than filled my soul in way that no food or drink could even begin to satisfy.

"The communist revolution came and went. Nothing seemed to change neither for us nor for anyone we knew. Daddy hated the communists but no one dared speak ill against them for fear losing their lives. Then came the Nazis and with them the fear of imprisonment and extermination. The Nazis pushed deep within our Country. The entire population of Russia was in upheaval. Panic ruled our days and those who could fled for safer lands. I was one of those who ran away from the Motherland. With my parents dead my only responsibility was to your Mother. I promised myself that I would not let your mother Irina die at an early age because of this senseless useless war.

"In 1942 with the little money that I had saved, and with a lot of luck your Mother and I found a passage out of Russia and to the relative safety of Shanghai. Many Russians also fled there during these turbulent years. We found refuge with those of our own kind and began a new life together".

 "Little by little we saved money and within a few years we started our own Bakery in a run-down area of Shanghai. This was my Papa's trade when he was still alive and I learned much as I would help him bake and even tend to the ovens. We catered to the local restaurants and we also baked traditional Russian dishes that we sold to the many of our countrymen in the area.

"It was also during this time that I met and fell in love with Victor. He was also a Russian immigrant who we would refer to more commonly as a Ladies Man as he was tall, strong, and virile. He was much younger than I but the difference in our age didn't seem to bother Victor and it certainly didn't bother me. When I was with him I always felt like I was a teenage girl again; young, carefree, and in love.

"It was the second year of my relationship with Victor that I awoke one day to find that my entire life savings had vanished and along with my savings. Victor too had vanished. The account I had with the local Merchants Bank had been emptied.

"Unable to pay my creditors and within a matter of weeks I was completely broke. I lost everything I owned including the Bakery. I also lost the man who I thought I would marry. The devastation of his abandonment and deceit would not be felt immediately but it would certainly leave its mark.

"Your Mother and I spoke frequently of moving to the United States. It was a dream we both had. I made the decision to leave. I felt that there was no better time than this to begin a new life. The move wouldn't be for a few months since I needed time to find work and save money for the trip"

"As the months passed a young stranger came into your Mother's Life. He was man of Portuguese descent. We learned that he too was an immigrant to China. His name was Leonard and he began to court your Mother in earnest. Soon they were inseparable and they began to speak of marriage.

"So having saved a modest amount of money the time soon came to depart China for the United States. Because of Leonard your Mother was reluctant to leave with me.

"Many arguments ensued and in the end I made the decision to leave for America alone. Your mother gave her solemn oath that she would soon follow.

"Alas with only the one bag I carried I arrived in America in 1951. It was a strange and frightening land. I had little money, no relatives, and no friends. To make matters worse I didn't speak a word of English. I finally made my way to San Francisco, California, were I decided to settle. I rented a small and dismal three-room apartment. Two egg crates were my only furnishings. My despair deepened. Unable to find steady work I did what I could to keep a roof over my head and to eat an occasional meal. I sought out other Russian immigrants, but found that they wanted nothing to do with me. I had been in America only four months when your Mother wrote telling me she had just married Leonard. She said that it might take a number of years, but they hoped that one day they would join me.

With tears in her eyes my Grandmother continued. I listened intently and felt her sorrow at a depth I didn't think possible.

"The letter from your Mother was more than I could bear. I felt betrayed, trapped, abandoned, and hopeless. That very same day I found a rope in a nearby maintenance closet near the front door to my apartment. I then fashioned one end of the rope into a noose. For hours I held that noose in my trembling hands. It was a cold and foggy San Francisco day. I sat staring out of the window and into the endless fog that poured over the mountains and into the city. My religious upbringing was such that by the mere entertainment of such a thought you could in fact be damned. I shuddered as I contemplated the unthinkable. My attention again shifted from the starkness of those empty lonely streets to the rope which I now held tightly in my sweating hands"

"With swift abandon I rose from my chair. I placed an egg crate below one of the ceiling beams that stretched the length of my living room. I stepped onto the crate and threw the rope over the beam. I tied off one end of the rope and placed the noose around my neck. I stepped off the crate. The rope tore at my throat, I gasped for air. I reached up with both hands and struggled to find space between the rope and my neck, but the rope was too tight. I kicked with both feet in a vain attempt to locate the egg crate. 'Let me find the crate I begged and I wouldn't do this again,' I screamed silently. I struggled for what seemed like an eternity. I felt myself slipping away.

"The next thing I realized, I was standing there watching this person dangling at the end of a rope. I saw that this person was in fact me! I watched as my legs kicked and within a short time, all movement stopped. I looked around my apartment and saw that there was a very bright light in the upper corner of the room. It shone with intensity of a spotlight. I knew that I must go into this light, but why? It also occurred to me that I was dead. I was fully aware of what had occurred.

"'But I'm still here' I thought.

"And this Kathryn is where my problems really began. In my mind I had committed the most awful and unforgivable of sins, I had taken my own life. The light that I was observing before me must surely be the pathway to Hell because I felt I deserved nothing less. I bolted toward my physical body that was now completely void of movement. I attempted to actually dive back into it but it was like running into a brick wall headfirst. It had to be the most utterly terrifying moment of my 'life.' I realized that up to this point in my miserable existence suicide was the absolute worst mistake I had ever made. All of the depression I had experienced while alive was still with me only now it was much worse. My 'Death' in fact changed nothing. It only magnified my problems into catastrophes the likes of which I never contemplated. I thought that my death was to be the end of my suffering but I was wrong.

"I again turned toward the light and found it still waiting for me. I knew that this light represented a doorway into another dimension but I felt it was a doorway to somewhere I did not wish to go. There was only one direction you could go in after committing such an act and it wasn't in the direction of Heaven. I bolted from the room and straight through the front door, and I do mean 'through' the front door. I found myself in the street and looking up toward my apartment and its front window. I wondered what would happen when they find my body.

"Kathryn, I can't begin to tell you how frightened I was. I looked for someone to call to. I felt that if my body were discovered in time I could be resuscitated. This would allow me to re-enter my body. I could get a second chance. If I were granted this I would never do anything this stupid again.

"Moments later I saw a car coming down the street. As it neared me I jumped into the middle of the road, waved my arms, and shouted 'Someone needs help!' The driver didn't even look in my direction as I braced for the impact of the car. To my astonishment there was no impact. He simply drove the car right through me. I was unhurt!

"This only makes sense, I remember thinking after all, I am 'dead.'

"I lingered on the sidewalk until darkness fell. With great trepidation I re-entered my apartment. After all I had nowhere else to go. The apartment was dark and as I drifted through the kitchen area I glanced toward the living room and its window. With the shades up the streetlights softly lit the interior of this small and barren room. Silhouetted against the window I could see my lifeless hanging body. I quickly looked away. I moved once again to the kitchen area and this is where I decided to remain.

She looked back into my eyes and continued. "It took them three days to find my body. Three days! And it was only because the rent was due. I watched them as they cut my body down, placed it in a sheet, and removed it from the apartment. They didn't know I was there. They sent a cleaning crew in next and readied the apartment for its new tenants. I remained in the kitchen. In the kitchen I was safe from the light. I couldn't see it from the kitchen and it couldn't see me, but it remained there silently lighting the corner of the room. I didn't trust this light. I felt like I knew where it led and I wasn't going to go there. I had already been through a mental and physical hell.

I stood silently as she continued her story. "During my time in the apartment I became the unseen guest of a number of people who would move in for a short while only to move out. Most of the 'renters' of the Apartment didn't know that I co-existed with them. I was very quiet you know. No one was truly aware that I was there.

No one knew I was there, except for one.

"His name was Billy and he moved in after two others had come and gone. Billy had long hair and wore beads. I found Billy to be very effeminate. He was nothing like any of the men I had known before. Most of Billy's time was spent in the kitchen area with me. He liked that kitchen. Billy also liked drugs, and so did his guests. At first I didn't realize what they were doing. But this wasn't the only thing that bewildered me. The new style of music they listened to shook me to my soul. I found its vibratory sensations very negative and distasteful. I couldn't believe that the world had come to this. How could they dare call this music? I was repulsed with their lifestyle. To me they were reprobates who only wanted to escape their lives.

"One evening, Billy who once again seated at the kitchen table, unexpectedly turned toward me and shouted 'Get out of here!' I looked around to see whom he was shouting at. He and I were the only ones in that room. Was he delirious from the Drugs or did he sense that he wasn't alone?

That same evening a guest arrived. He looked very much like Billy, sporting long hair and a beard. 'Dirty looking,' I remembered telling myself, he was very dirty looking. Billy and his friend seated themselves at the table. Billy began telling him how he has been getting this 'creepy' feeling lately as though he was being watched. I felt myself freeze. Could he be referring to me? But his friend only laughed and the subject was changed much to my delight by the way for I wanted no one to know I was there. But Billy knew I was there, somehow he knew I was there.

Billy seemed to become more and more aware of my presence in that kitchen. Over time his periodic displeasure in my presence turned to verbal abuse. He now spent most of his time yelling and cursing at me, demanding that I leave.

On the last day of my 'hell' on Earth, Billy who had been gone most of the day returned early that evening. He was whistling as he entered the apartment. Walking into the kitchen it was obvious that he was in a very good mood. In hand he held a paper bag that he set down on the table. I was relieved by his apparent happiness and felt that perhaps on this night there would be no profane utterances and demands that I leave my Apartment. I had become deathly afraid of Billy recently. Perhaps Billy had had a change of heart.

Billy seated himself and began to construct his "cigarette" Billy referred to this type of cigarette as a Joint. He then lit it and inhaled deeply. Billy then reached for the paper bag that he placed on the table earlier. He reached inside and extracted a leafy brown plant like material that filled the palm of his hand. He placed this material in a large ashtray. He lit another match and placed the match to the material. The leafy substance began to burn. Billy then blew it out. The material then began emitting large volumes of smoke as it smoldered. The smoke began to fill the kitchen. Billy rose from his chair, grabbed the ashtray from the table and began walking through the apartment with it. As he walked he laughed in a sarcastic tone. I wondered what he could be doing. 'Had he lost his mind?' I wondered.

"Billy re-entered the kitchen and placed the still smoldering ashtray on the table. 'I want you out of here' he screamed. 'Get out of my apartment' he yelled. 'Your apartment?' I thought. 'This is my apartment, I died here!'

"Like a whirling Dervish Billy began to spin wildly in the middle of the kitchen. I panicked and moved to the opposite corner as he continued to spin. With both arms outstretched as he spun he lost his balance and fell against the kitchen sink. I made a dash for the opposite side of the room. Billy quickly regained his balance and grabbed a large cast iron skillet that sat nearby. 'Dear God someone please help me' I screamed. He must have heard me because with that utterance and with all his might Billy swung the skillet directly toward my head. I quickly jumped out of the way and ran into the living room area. I was in such a panic it didn't even occur to me that the thing I feared most, the tunnel still awaited me only a few feet away.

"Like a scared rabbit I huddled in the corner of the living room. In the kitchen I could hear glass breaking and things being thrown about. 'Please someone help me' I prayed. Just then, a voice said to me; 'Kathryn, come with me and you will be safe.' As I looked up I beheld an outstretched arm reaching for my hand. The hand belonged to my Mother. I joined my hand to hers and the rest you can guess.

"I didn't go up a tunnel like you Kathryn. I simply, and suddenly, found myself 'on the other side.'"

With all the wisdom of the Universe within her and a look in her eyes that only spoke of bliss she continued.

"My darling Kathryn, I experienced those things that most people do when they pass. I met all of my relatives who were there to greet me on this side. You know it was like attending the most wonderful reunion you could possibly imagine. I was also given a life review. For me this was the hardest part. And now... well now I wait to go back to try it again."

"But Grandma there are some things I still don't understand," I pleaded. Pointedly she continued.

"We judge ourselves Kathryn, no one else judges us. When I took my own life I believed because of what I was taught all my life that I was doomed to hell through eternity. It wasn't until I reached out for help that I was given it and therefore I was guided into the right direction. But the decision to take my own life was the wrong one. I realized this as soon I did it.

"God gives us the greatest blessing in the Universe: the gift of soul growth with the Earth plane as his finest testing grounds. It is a contract that our higher self agrees to enter into. We leave here with the understanding that we must stay the course and ride out the time that is allotted us during this life. Souls will incarnate into absolute destitution only to starve to death as children all for the chance to elevate its experience. It matters not that this experience is brief and brutal. The soul will grasp at any opportunity to participate. It is this precious. We make the mistake of thinking that the physical plane is the only reality. I also made this mistake.

"Those of us who take their own lives have in effect broken the contract. We falsely believe this will be the end of our suffering. Believe me it is not. Nothing changes. You will find yourself in the same position once again facing the same problems, the same hopelessness. It is your mission to get through these rough times. This is how we grow. And certainly you can make it through because as it has been said, you are never given more than you can handle. So if you are facing such a dismal time in your life the kind I faced you can rest assured that you could make it through because eventually you must make it through. I can only hope that when I am once again given the same sort of life hurdles I can on this occasion find the strength to succeed.

"Let me tell you a little of what I have learned", she said.

"The Earth plane is reality, but it is only one reality because there are many. If it can be conceived of and visualized it is a reality. For those without the eyes to see and ears to hear it becomes their only reality, their only possibility. This universe plane is but one. There are also many universes all made up of vibratory light and all that is comes from thought. These universes are also layered. What separates and makes distinct each layer is its vibratory state.

"The Earth and the universe in which it exist were designed to appear real. The universe is holographic in nature complete with endless stimuli that dance upon your senses and invoke your imagination. Devoid of all memories before birth, most of us assume that this is all there is. Reality is a perfect illusion and within this illusion we are allowed to participate and co-create within the illusion. The Grand Master created the laws of our reality. In science we call these immutable laws Psychics. It is within the parameters of these laws that we are allowed to 'create,' because first there must be structure, and before this structure came Him. He and His laws are perfect."

"Had I known these truths perhaps things may have ended differently for me. But I have been given another chance and for this I am grateful beyond words".

"Darling Kathryn, I have been sent to help guide you through all of this. But first you must go through a life review as did I and I will help you through this. If at any time you need help you are only to call out for me."

"A life review?" I asked.

"Let me explain it to you" she said as she placed her right hand on my shoulder.

"During your life review you will feel the presence and renewed experience of not only every act but also every thought from your life up to this point. You will realize that all of it is an energy field that influences one as well as others. All that has been done and thought will seem to be significant and it is all recorded. Insight will be obtained about whether love was given or on the contrary withheld. Because you are connected with the memories, emotions, and the consciousness of another person, you experience the consequences of your own thoughts, words, and actions. Therefore during your life review you will understand that there is a connection with the fields of consciousness of other persons as well as with your own fields of consciousness. There is interconnectedness. You will observe your entire life in one glance. Time and space will not seem to exist during this experience.

"But I'm not finished", she continued.

"All of your life up till the present will seem to be placed before you in a kind of panoramic three-dimensional review and each event will seem to be accompanied by a consciousness of good or evil or with an insight into cause and effect. Not only will you perceive everything from your own viewpoint, but you will also know the thoughts of everyone involved in the event as if you had their thoughts within you. This means that you will perceive not only what you have done and thought, but also the way in which it influenced others. At all times during the review the importance of love will be emphasized. Your review may feel like a long time because every subject will come up, but at the same time it may seem like just a fraction of a second because you will perceive it all at the same moment. Time and distance will not seem to exist. You will be in all places at the same time, and sometimes your attention will be drawn to something and then you will be present there.

"But for you Kathryn, your life review will be a little different from most, since your time here is limited and you must go back. Your life review will take place back on the Earth plane itself. During this time you may speed up your review or you may slow it down. You may also completely relive it as if it were happening to you again. But at all times you will be deeply aware of the effects of your actions, inactions, and each and every word you uttered and its affect on others.

"Also, a preview may examined, in which both future images from your personal life events as well as more general images from the future might occur to you even though it must be stressed that these perceived images should be considered purely as possibilities. Some people refer to this affect as Déjà Vu. Again it will seem as if time and space do not exist during your review. Let me explain this to you in a different way.

"I am going to tell you something and I want you to think about this and remember it. When you are out of the physical, time as you know it does not exist. There is no time out of the physical because you consist of light, and as a light being you are in fact moving at the speed of light. At the speed of physical light there is no time. So when you go back into the body and remember that it felt like there was no time here you will understand."

Smiling, she looked at me. I could tell she was pleased that she could impart such wisdom to me. It was as though she bestowed upon me the greatest gift. Of course it was the greatest gift that one could give to another, it was a gift of love.

"Interesting," I thought, but I still wasn't ready for a life review.

I knew I hadn't been perfect, but to review every aspect of my life - every word uttered and how those words or actions or in-actions drastically affected those near me and even changed the course of their lives - would overwhelm me. I wasn't eager to wit-ness these spiritual trespasses.

"But I was told I was going back. Why then am I to have a life review?" I pleaded.

My Grandmother smiled once again and said "Kathryn, this a gift that is being given to you. You must accept it. It will not be painful for you it is not a punishment. You will only be enlight-ened by it. Do I not love you? Haven't I always loved you? If this is so then you must trust in me."

Indeed it was so. I have always loved her. I trusted her with every fiber of my being. I realized that I had known her since the beginning of time. I also knew that our relationship would con-tinue in many forms, many guises, and would span the length of time itself.

"Turn around Kathryn. Look at that big wonderful ball of blue in all its splendid majesty. It is but a learning center. Look closely Kathryn, look closely and remember" I turned once again and looked Earthward.

CHAPTER THREE

A Return to Earth

As I looked downward the Earth began to move toward me. Faster and faster I rushed forward. The stars flew past me and everything became a blur. Instinctively I braced for an impact.

Suddenly I stopped. I found myself floating over the planet. I wasn't very high. Looking down I could see the contours of land. The land was surrounded by water on three sides. "I knew this place," I thought. It was San Francisco, I was born here. To the North I could see the Golden Gate Bridge as it spanned its way to Marin County. To the West I could see the Pacific Ocean. To the East was the San Francisco Bay. I felt a sense of relief.

As I watched I could feel the wind gently pushing me from side to side. The temperature felt perfect. I drifted like a bird. It then occurred to me that perhaps I could even maneuver like a bird. I decided I wanted to move right. By simply thinking this I began to move right. I then decided to move left and I moved left. I thought of moving up and up I went. "Let's move lower for a closer look," I thought.

I began to move down toward the Earth. "Faster," I thought.

The ground began to move ever faster toward me. "Stop" I yelled, and I stopped. I was now perhaps a thousand feet above the City.

As I floated there I could quite clearly see all of the neat little homes and the streets that the homes sat adjacent to. In the streets I could see that cars were moving up and down and through intersections. Though quite small I could also observe people walking on the sidewalks. To my left was a schoolyard and I could see that children were at play.

"I must get closer," I thought. But then a thought occurred to me: what if the people see me? What then? But no one looks up, people don't look up, they are too engrossed in this box they have created, this limited reality, complete with visual and mental parameters. "I was safe and if they do see me I can just fly away," I reasoned. This put my mind at rest and I glanced downward again.

I ventured ever closer to the ground. I stopped near the top of the telephone poles. Two passing cars caught my attention. There was nothing so unusual about these cars other than the fact that they were very old cars with new paint. They looked to be in a fairly new condition. I looked about even more and saw that the cars that were parked nearby were also vintage cars. "How could this be?" I wondered. I then recalled seeing older black and white movies where all of these cars were of a certain period. The movie American Graffiti came to mind. These cars looked like the cars in American Graffiti, but maybe even older. I must investigate this further I thought.

I looked up and down the street. To my left I could see large office type skyscrapers in the distance. I would go left. I outstretched both my arms like a bird and began flying toward the downtown area. From the rooftop level I glided down the center of the street following its twists and turns. I delighted and reveled in my new-found freedom of flight. I could go anywhere in the twinkling of an eye. I was experiencing unadulterated blissful freedom the likes of which I had never felt before. I was free of the physical body with all of its encumbrances. It occurred to me that I could sense some things almost on a physical level. There was no pain of any sort, no hunger, no anxiety, and no want other than the craving for knowledge. Knowledge and the answer to my deepest questions is what motivated me.

As I flew closer to the downtown area I decided I would slow down and have a better look at the scene below. Near the center of the financial district I decided to stop at a large intersection. As I came to a standstill and floated but feet above the street I once again noted that the cars were all dated, very dated. The people who were all in a great hurry appeared dressed much differently also. The style of the suits and the dresses that the ladies wore were of a very old fashion.

A sudden wave of realization struck me. Somehow I was returned to an earlier time on Earth, a time much earlier than when I had left.

"I must be in the 50's!" I said to myself.

I had to find a way to verify the time I was in. As I looked around I noticed that there were newspaper stands on all the corners of the intersection. As soon as I thought "I must go to one," I was suddenly there standing in front of it.

The newspapers were enclosed in a metal dispenser. A dirty plastic cover allowed one to preview its contents. I moved forward again and I looked for a date. In the upper right hand corner was the edition date: August 25th, 1958. Stunned I turned from the news rack and focused again on the people rushing past me. Indeed it all made sense now. I was back in time.

"Why should this shock me?" I thought. Certainly after all this nothing should shock me anymore!

Just then and right behind me, an impatient angry driver began blowing his horn incesentanly. Without willing it and like a rocket I was launched into the sky above. Higher I went until I had to consciously will myself to stop. Once again I found myself above the City and safe from its insanity.

From my vantage point I was able see across San Francisco and to the Pacific Ocean. It was in this area of San Francisco that I spent my childhood.

With both arms outstretched I began flying toward the ocean. The buildings and streets below rushed past me.

As I grew closer to the Ocean areas below me began to look familiar. I slowed myself and began to look for specific landmarks. Nearby I could see the main thoroughfare that I traveled so many times with my parents. Not far from there was the Catholic Church we attended. Near that sat the elementary school I spent many happy years in.

It then occurred to me that I would find the house that I spent my first thirteen years. After all it was only but a few blocks from my school. "Where is it?" I thought to myself. I continued to scan the area and was unable to locate the house. Frustration began to turn to panic.

"I want to go home!" I yelled. With that utterance and in the blink of an eye I found myself hovering directly over the house of my childhood. From this viewpoint I starred downwards. I was able to see the closely manicured and perfectly kept garden in the front of the house. I looked over and could see the backyard. Though filled with children's toys the backyard was immaculate and perfectly trimmed with everything perfectly in its place. Seeing this I chuckled to myself. After all my Father epitomized the word "perfectionist" and everything about the house was indeed perfect; its paint, its roof, its lawn, and even the street in front of the house was free of any debris or apparent disorder.

A host of thoughts raced through my mind at that moment. Childhood nostalgia began to fill my heart. Recollections of horror and fear also began to fill me. I was torn with unbearable emotion.

Almost imperceptibly I found myself being pulled toward the roof of the house. "What's happening now?" I blurted out. "Stop" I said. It was of no use, I was being pulled toward the house and there was nothing I could do about it.

Suddenly there was a "whooshing" noise and I suddenly found myself in my physical body. I was in fact in my infancy. Physically I was only days old. I wondered what I could possibly gain from reliving this period of my life. I wanted to go forward in my life to a time when I was physically mobile not a helpless infant. My wish came true and time accelerated. The days flew by and I quickly and instantly relived each and every very boring moment of my very early childhood. I stopped my age progression and went to "real time."

As I looked about, I slowly began to recognize many of the things within the room. In the corner was my first bed, and on the bed next to the pillow was my favorite stuffed animal - a nameless, tattered, brown and white stuffed dog. On my dresser was a black and white picture of me sitting in the lap of an unsmiling Santa Claus. In the other corner was my miniature rocking chair. As I gazed about I recognized a familiar voice calling out.

"Kathryn, I won't tell you again! Get in here!"

Without thinking I turned toward the door leading to the hallway and reached for the door. I was able to see a physical hand reaching for the knob. I stopped and looked down at my right hand, I then looked at my left. I was certainly physical again. I turned and ran to the three quarter length mirror hanging from my closet door. It appeared to me I was five years old.

And then a voice rang out from down the hallway; "Kathryn, I won't tell you again!" It was my Mother and her now demanding and frightful voice sent shudders through my little body. Instinctually I turned from the mirror and ran toward the door.

"How strange it felt to be back in the physical" I thought. Yes strange, not only to be back in the physical, but also to be back in the body of a five year old! I turned once again and bolted through the door and ran down the hallway turning at the corner of the hall and darting into the kitchen where my Mother was waiting.

Hardly able to contain myself I blurted out, "Mama, I'm back!"

"Back from where?" was my Mothers response.

"But mama I was gone for such a long time and now I have come back!"

"Kathryn, when I call you better come. Now what is this nonsense with you having been gone? Gone where?" she asked again.

My exuberance had now subsided and I struggled to get hold of myself. I felt that if my response to this question evoked anger from my Mother then I would surely pay for it. Of this I was sure.

I chose silence.

I found it fascinating that I was in fact completely reliving this time in my life replete with familiar surroundings and a physical body. I never imagined it would be this way. It was completely inter-active.

But why was I flung into this particular time. What was so important about this period? Why did I instinctively choose to stop at this period in life?

There was one other thing that nagged at the back of my mind. The experience I was having was so overwhelming and powerful that I felt my emotions and even my thoughts were changing or reverting back to an earlier time. I was now struggling to retain my adult mental state. I felt that a part of me was slipping away. There seemed to be a meshing of two people within me, one an adult, the other a child and both fully aware of each other. One moment I would be fully emerged in a situation with the mental capabilities and understanding of the particular age or time that I found myself in. In the next moment I was mentally detached from the situation, examining it and learning from it as an adult. I found that I could slide in and out of both states.

My Mother who was busy stirring a pot on the stove looked around at me and asked, "Have you cleaned up your room Kathryn? You know your Father doesn't like a messy room?"

Unsure of the state of my bedroom meekly I answered; "Yes mommy".

"Well you better make sure it's straightened up because your Father will be home any minute and you don't want to make him mad, do you?"

"No mommy" was my reply.

I turned and walked to my bedroom. With much trepidation I opened the door to my room. I spent the better part of the next half hour sitting on my bed petting my stuffed dog and starring out the window. Lost in thought I neglected my Mother's instructions to straighten the room.

As if in a state of hypnosis I sat transfixed. I remembered Einstein's quote with those words repeating in my mind over and over again.

"Quite a thought for a five year old" I thought. Surely Einstein knew the secrets of the universe and shared these ideas with us. How many grasped the truth of these words and was it really necessary that we understand these things while experiencing the "earthly plane" Perhaps during this brief period in time it isn't really necessary for us to grasp these realities. Perhaps we are better off not knowing these realities. Just maybe our lessons are better served in this "unknowingness".

Thoughts of my childhood raced through my mind. I reflected on this specific moment of my life and how it had been full of love, a love that was bestowed upon me by loving a loving family. This was a good time in my life, but I also knew, and remembered, that the tranquility of this time was about to change for the worse.

My concentration was broken by the sound of a car door closing in the driveway. I leaned toward the window and pulled back the sheer curtains that obscured my view.

It was my Father who was now hurriedly removing packages from the backseat of his new car. My Father changed cars as regularly as some people change underwear. He was never satisfied with the status quo. He didn't "keep up with the Jones's"; he was the Jones's!

As I watched I wondered what type of mood he would be in tonight. Certainly it all depended on how his day was at work. If it was a good day then his mood reflected this. If it were a bad day then all of us paid for it that night.

My Father Leonard was from the old country and he was assuredly old fashioned in everything he did and thought. Hard working and hard-nosed he left Portugal with the intent of fulfilling the American dream and nothing was going to stop him.

Leonard learned the real estate business quickly and opened up his own brokerage. My Father was intelligent, complex, driven, and a very talented man. While a youth in Portugal he was gifted in Soccer and could have gone professional. He also excelled in music having mastered many instruments. Looking back it seemed his life was indeed contradictory.

But even a rose is flawed. One of my Father's characteristics included an exaggerated and obsessive compulsion to succeed.

The drive to succeed was coupled with acute impatience that often turned to rage. In the Psychological Field they call one of his peculiarities "redirected aggression". Leonard would vent his anger upon the closest person. For Leonard there was always an unwilling victim nearby. The most important thing for my Father was his ability to vent when needed and this need arose with great regularity. Leonard had great intensity and this intensity was manifested in all that he did.

Physically my Father was a small man. I often wondered if this wasn't the foundation of his extremes. Like many of us he was frightened and insecure.

Naturally at the age of five years I was not aware of this. I only knew that he was my Father and I loved him. To this day I still love him. Leonard was a profane man and much of his profanity was directed at me. Why then was I the centerpiece to his emotional storms. I have no answers to this riddle. Perhaps it is this unknowing that tortures me the most.

But on this night the verbal abuse escalated for the first time into physical abuse that was sadistic in manner and protracted in duration. Again it was I who was the focus of his new tactics.

The silence of my room was interrupted when my older sister Cynthia burst through my door. "Kathy, it's dinner time! Come on!" Cynthia left my door ajar, then turned and disappeared down the hallway in direction of the kitchen.

Cynthia was six years older than me and very grown up. I felt no kinship with her and she pretty much avoided me whenever she could. My only contact with her was at dinnertime or on Sundays when it was traditional for the whole family to take drives through the Marin County countryside.

Cynthia was my Father's favorite and this was no secret to anyone including my Mother who chose to ignore the obvious difference. Cynthia sat at the top of the heap within the pecking order that included my older brother Rob.

Rob was intelligent, precocious, and strong-willed. I don't think my Father knew exactly what to make of Rob, nor how to handle him. Mostly my Father left him alone. Rob found himself somewhere between my Fathers love of Cynthia and his hatred of me. Certainly Rob wasn't in a bad position. His was one of partial anonymity with little interaction with my Father.

Rob and I were close friends and playmates. I turned to him when I needed a friend. As Rob and I matured both intellectually and emotionally we seemed to develop along parallel lines in terms of interests and preoccupations. Certainly for brothers and sisters this may come as no surprise. But as Rob and I grew into adulthood we would also share an intense disdain for a man who could have had our highest respect but who choose quite intentionally to destroy the love and all the positive accompanying emotions that a child has for his or her parent.

More importantly our Father changed the course of our lives. He was a man of great talents, but he was also a man who delighted in imprisoning our spirit and repressing our growth.

My Mother once again called for me. Slowly I rose from my bed hesitant to leave the security of my room. I slowly walked to the kitchen only to be "greeted" by the silent malevolent stare of my

Father who was already seated.

I took my designated position at the table as Cynthia seated herself beside me.

With deliberate exaggeration Cynthia placed a paper napkin on her lap, positioning it perfectly, then patting it once. Looking up and across the table she smiled at my Father.

"Good evening Daddy how was your day?"

"It could have been better, but thank you for asking. And how was yours Cynthia?"

"I had a wonderful day daddy" was her reply, forcing an exaggerated smile.

Our attention now turned to the hallway. From his room Rob was running at full speed toward the kitchen. I chuckled to myself finding it quite funny. Rob always made me laugh. Bursting into the kitchen Rob almost lost his balance as he came to a sliding stop on the spotlessly clean floor.

My Father slammed his fist to the kitchen table and screamed at Rob "You bloody donkey is that any way to enter the room?"

Rob quickly took his seat refusing to answer or acknowledge my Fathers rebuke.

My Mother silently and diligently placed the food on the table and quickly seated herself. We all hung our heads, closed our eyes, and clasped our hands in preparation for prayer that my Father always led us in. We were a Catholic Family and Father insured that we kept true to our faith. No one questioned any of the daily ceremonies and rituals. Certainly it was something that we all felt good about. It gave us comfort and reassurance.

My Father ended the prayer and in perfect unison we all raised our heads. Obediently my Mother passed the meat dish to my Father as my brother and sister began filling their plates with side dishes.

Finally breaking her silence my Mother asked me if I had straightened my room as she requested.

"No mama", I stuttered.

"Why not?" my Father asked.

I stared blankly at my Father. Anger filled his eyes. Frozen with fear and searching for an answer I returned his stare unable to speak.

"What are you looking at you bloody little cow I told you not to stare at me with those eyes of yours!" he said loudly.

My Father adjusted his position on his chair and leaned toward me saying, "She's a bloody witch"

I didn't see it coming, but suddenly I found myself being hurled off my chair. My Father had slapped me across the face. I weighed perhaps thirty-five pounds, but with the ferocity of his slap it was enough to send me flying into the air and onto the floor.

This was the first time my Father struck me, but as I well knew it certainly wouldn't be the last.

Needless to say I was in shock. The blow itself didn't hurt, not right away that is. I struggled to come to my senses. As I opened my eyes I saw that my Brother was kneeling beside me calling my name.

"Take the bloody witch to her bedroom" were my Father's instructions to Rob.

Rob brought me to my feet and with his arm around me he slowly walked me to my bedroom.

I spent the next hour in my room sobbing uncontrollably. I was in such emotional distress that I once again failed to clean up my room as instructed and for this indiscretion I would pay dearly.

The door to my room swung open and my Father entered. He placed both hands on his hips as he stood in the doorway.

"Why didn't you clean this room up like I told you to?" he screamed.

In two steps he covered the distance of the room from the door to where I was laying on the bed. With his left hand he grabbed my right arm and pulled me off the bed. He began slapping me across the face with his right hand shouting "Why, why, why?"

I began calling out for my Mother, but she didn't come. My Mother never came.

I am not sure how many times my Father slapped me, but I thought the abuse and the madness of this moment would never end. I felt I would be beaten to death.

An eternity passed and he released his grasp. I fell to the floor. He grew tired of striking me, or, perhaps a moment of sanity overcame him. Whatever the reason I was happy to be free of this violent little man who I could only perceive as a monster.

My perception of the world at that moment changed. This incident would "color" the way I viewed and reacted to every circumstance in my life from this point forward. A Godly innocence was wrenched from me in the span of but a few moments. I could never reclaim this part of me, at least not in this lifetime.

I opened my eyes and starred at him in disbelief. Defiantly I lashed out at him.

"I hate you!"

I think I was more shocked than he. What was this emotion that caused me to say these words? The emotion of hatred was foreign to me. Certainly I had never had these feelings before. It was an epiphany of sorts, an earth-shattering event in my life. One I would never forget.

My Father appeared frozen in time. There was a perceptible change in his eyes. His mouth hung open and he appeared confused and in deep reflection. Hysterically I began to cry. The pain in my facial area began to manifest and spread through my entire head.

Suddenly waves of sadness and rejection began to overwhelm me. It began slowly at first and increased in severity. I thought at first these were my own feelings, a result of the beating I had just survived.

With concerted effort I gained control of myself. I stopped crying and attempted to make sense of all this.

I looked toward him once again and could now see that he and I were connected by the same shimmering thread of light that I remembered seeing earlier during my "death" in the operating room. The thread of light extended from my Fathers solar plexus region and attached itself to me in the same area.

My attention shifted as images began flooding into my mind. Unrecognizable scenes of a foreign land and unrecognizable people speaking a foreign tongue danced in my consciousness. The general feeling that engulfed me was negative and heart wrenching. I was engulfed with feelings of unworthiness, rejection and scorn.

I quickly understood that I was glimpsing snippets of my Father's life. I saw them, I heard them, and I lived them as he did. My identity disappeared as I assumed his. I felt everything he felt at that moment.

The words "I hate you" ostensibly opened a floodgate of resentment and self-hatred that festered within my Father all of his life. It made no difference that these words were just, or that he deserved them. One might reason that a small beaten child spoke these words. None of this mattered in the scheme of things. All that mattered is that the words were said and the effects were the same.

The words cut through my Father like a cold knife. But what is more important to understand is that these words also tore through me in a like manner. A self-inflicted wound you might say.

I felt extreme remorse for what I had said. My own words hurt me as much or perhaps more than they had hurt him. I was in deep sorrow for both of us. The sorrow I felt wasn't simply due to the effect that the words had. I felt a deep regret that those words could come from me. It was a blending of sorrows for multiple reasons.

I picked myself up from the floor and ran to my Father.

I jumped into my Fathers arms and told him I didn't mean what I said. I asked for his forgiveness. I told him I loved him.

My Father returned my embrace, holding me limply. With my face touching his I could feel the tears from his eyes streaming down his cheeks and onto mine. I looked into his eyes once again searching for any glimmer of love or tenderness, but there was none.

"Get into your pajamas, it's time for bed" was his only response. He lowered me to the floor, slowly turned, and walked out of my room.

I once again began to weep uncontrollably. My emotional state was indescribable because this time I not only wept for myself, but I also wept for him.

CHAPTER FOUR

A Familiar Spectre

Exhausted and broken I lay my head down on my pillow and cuddled with my stuffed dog. The pain of the abuse administered by my Father was still with me. My head throbbed. Despite this I slowly began to drift into sleep. Once again my mind was flooded with scenes of the past.

I was leaving this period or cycle in my life and being thrust forward into time.

My childhood raced before me. Images materialized then vanished and new ones appeared. I absorbed and sifted through millions of seconds, minutes, and hours, reliving in a flash all that I was all that I experienced and becoming one with the emotion of all who were affected by me.

Although I was both completely involved in my recall I was at the same time detached from it observing it as if from afar like a scientist peering through a microscope.

I wondered if it were possible once again to slow this process down or inversely speed it up? I decided I would try. What the heck I thought. I possess all the time in the world or more precisely, the illusion of time did not exist for me while in this state. I decided I would take advantage of this.

I willed myself forward in time. The scenes of my life rushed by. I decided to experiment. I would slow things down.

"Slow down" I commanded

To my amazement everything began to slow. I found that I was able to adjust the flow of recall or data as one would on today's computers when one downloads files or programs.

The scenes drifted by slowly now. I concentrated on the time period and found that I was in my very early teens. I found myself at the age of thirteen. This was not a particularly bad time in my life. I was no longer a child nor was I yet an adult.

During this period I was also better equipped to defend myself both mentally and physically.

"Perhaps I should slow this down a little further" I thought.

Instantaneously my mental screen went dark. There were no more images to observe. For a brief moment it was as though I was blinded, nonexistent, tossed into a void of nothingness where all sensory stimuli ceased to exist.

Then quite suddenly and much to my relief I became aware of a dim light all about me. The light grew in intensity. I was regaining my sight. It was as though the sun were coming up displacing the despair of darkness and disconnection. Within moments I had full vision again. My bedroom began to come into focus, but it was not the same bedroom that I had just left.

This room was larger and light beige color. The furnishings too were different. I looked about and discovered that my stuffed dog was still on my bed. This was the only thing I recognized. I stood up and went to the window. Looking out I could see that my surroundings were different also.

"Amazing" I thought. "I'm in the Burlingame house."

I glanced around once again and found the same mirror that hung from the door in the old house was now hanging from the closet door in this one. I smiled as I stepped toward the mirror. I now beheld myself many years older than I was on my previous "stop" in time.

Though only in my late twenties when I "died" I had become keenly cognizant of the wrinkles and signs of aging that were beginning to manifest at that time.

"How wonderful" I exclaimed. I stepped closer to the mirror and examined what was now a wrinkle free face. I stepped away from the mirror again and slowly turned from side to side drinking in the vibrancy of youth.

"I believe I will stay here a while" I thought.

My Father never being content with what he had decided in the mid-sixties that he would move the family to the peninsula of San Francisco. Burlingame was a twenty-minute drive south of San Francisco and was your basic suburban bedroom community. Today they call this area the northern tip of Silicon Valley; we came to refer to this area as "Siberia."

My Father was the only one content with the relocation. The bigger and better house certainly suited his ego. My Mother who was always obedient and subservient to my Father simply went along with the program as always.

My siblings too had mixed emotions with the move. Cynthia lost her friends also, but since Father was happy she was willing to endure any personal hardship. Rob too suffered but he was highly adaptable and very supportive to everyone during this transition. But there was a new addition to the family since my earlier "stop-over" and he was named Stephen Francis Doss.

Steve was born in 1962 and quickly became everyone's favorite. Bright and witty Steve and I became fast friends often sharing our misadventures and the inevitable retribution of our Father.

But I for one still considered myself a San Franciscan as I think we all did. As far as I was concerned there was nothing here on the peninsula for me. I had been uprooted from my familiar sur-roundings, was forced to become estranged from my friends, and felt I had lost contact with the "civilized world".

Despite this I made friends quickly and excelled in school and sports. Many of my friends were also San Francisco transplants so we had much in common.

Making friends for me was never a problem. For some reason people simply opened up to me. Perfect strangers would approach me and within a few minutes I would know their entire life story. Although I often wondered why this was, I always welcomed it, then and now.

As I peered out my bedroom window and into a beautiful sum-mer day the ringing of the telephone jolted me. Instinctively I knew who it was. I quickly reached for the phone

"Hi Deana, what's up?"

"How did you know it was me again Kathy?" she laughed.

"I just knew," I said.

Deana paused, and in a more serious tone said; "I think your Father is right you are a witch."

Those words actually hurt me. I wasn't going to let Deana know how deeply it hurt and I really didn't know why they hurt. Perhaps it was because my Father used that word to humiliate me. Or perhaps I was a witch.

It was true that I was very sensitive to others. I would only have to look at someone and I would know instantly if they were experiencing a problem and what that problem was. I didn't know how I knew I simply knew.

This ability of course enamored me to my girlfriends. They would often come to me when they were experiencing a problem with their parents, school, or more importantly with a boyfriend or would-be boyfriend. I counseled them and gave them advice and direction. I was seldom wrong.

I accomplished these readings by simply looking into their eyes. Or if they were curious about someone who wasn't present then all I would need was a picture of that person. They were all an open book and I found it quite easy to "read" anyone, anyone except those closest to me. The closer someone was to me the harder it was for me to read that person. This was especially true for myself. I found it almost impossible to discern my own future.

I found all of this quite natural and often wondered why others didn't possess the same abilities. I truly cared about people, and wanted to help them. I was aware that I had a gift from God, and I wanted to share this with others in the same fashion that you would share your meal with a hungry friend. I was giving a part of me to them and through this, I was also nourished. It made me feel complete.

Deana and I decided to meet at the usual meeting spot, an intersection about three blocks from my house.

Within minutes I stood waiting for Deana. Closing my eyes I felt the warmth of the sun and the gentle ocean breeze caressing my skin and hair. It was good to be alive and it was a wonderful time of my life. I drank in every moment.

Deana arrived and we decided to sit cross-legged in the middle of the sidewalk as we discussed what we would do next.

It was Deana who saw him first.

"Who is that guy?" Deana asked.

"What guy?" I replied.

Looking up I could see an old and scraggly man standing directly across the street from us. He stood there silently and seemingly transfixed on us.

The appearance of this specter was sudden as neither Deana nor myself saw where he came from.

Almost inaudibly Deana asked; "Have you ever seen him before?"

I didn't respond to her question and instead I continued to stare back at this threatening figure. I felt he was staring directly at me. Incredibly he seemed vaguely familiar.

"This guy looks like a child molester Kathy we better run," said Deana.

I responded to Deana's pleading by explaining to her that I

thought I recognized this old man. As I locked eyes with this strange grotesque man an indescribable fear began to well up within me. A mixture of fear and curiosity was immobilizing me now.

Deana screamed out; "Oh my God Kathy look at his right hand"

I looked to where his right hand should have been, but in its place was a metal hook! His coat covered his right arm to the wrist and from this the silver colored hook extended outwards. He held the hook close to his body. The opposite hand he kept in the pocket of his coat.

Appearing to be about seventy years of age he stood there motionless. Leaning slightly forward he appeared almost hunch-backed. He wore an old fashioned black hat with a wide brim. The brim was pulled down around his ears and covered his eyebrows. His nose was sharply pointed and he appeared unshaven and dirty. He wore a dark and wrinkled trench coat that stretched well below his knees. His pants were also dark and his shoes appeared old and tattered.

"He looks like an undertaker," I whispered.

The terror of the moment was broken when Deana whispered to me that we should run for our lives. Leaning closer to Deana I remarked that during this entire time not once did I see him move.

Deana agreed adding; "He doesn't even blink!"

"Okay" I said. "We will both get up together and run straight for my house"

No sooner did I say this and we were both on our feet and

in a full sprint running as only terrified thirteen year olds could run. Having run almost a block I reached out toward Deana and grabbed her arm forcing her to slow down.

"Where is he now?" I said.

Deana and I looked back to where the man had been standing, but he was gone. With a few more searching glances up and down the street we assured ourselves that the threat was over.

Simultaneously we turned to each other and burst out laughing.

"Let's go," I said.

We turned once again and began to walk the remaining two blocks to my house. The casualness of our walk reflected the relief we felt. Neither of us spoke but as we walked our speed increased until once again we were in a full run.

Moments later we were in front of my house. In three or four bounds I cleared the thirteen steps that lead up to my front door. Deana followed close behind as I pushed opened the front door. We rushed in quickly slamming and locking the door behind us.

Once again we turned to each and laughed uncontrollably.

We spent the rest of the day within the confines and safety of the house. We didn't speak of that despicable old man again. I suppose the very thought of him disturbed and rattled our sanity, disrupting our reality.

The hours passed and as the dinner hour approached Deanna left for home. I said goodbye to her at the front door and as I turned to walk toward my room. Through the living room windows I could see Deanna running at full speed down the sidewalk. I chuckled to myself secure in the fact that I was safe within my house, untouchable, or so I thought.

I sat on the couch and stared out the front window contemplating the events of the day. A few minutes passed when I noticed my Father's car pulling into the driveway. My Father was at the wheel with my Mother-sitting close by. Normally the sight of my Father coming home did not evoke positive feelings within me but on this night I was delighted to see him.

My parents never spent time with me or my brothers and sister. If there was a free moment or day they mainly spent their time with each other. Their social life with friends was a busy one. There was always a party to attend or a social event on the calendar. Except for the occasional Sunday drives our parents shared no part of their lives with us and we shared none with them. During school functions or sporting events when other kids had their parents in attendance our Father and Mother were always conspicuously absent.

This hurt us all very deeply.

There were many things I didn't understand. My father of course made no secret that he regretted ever having us. My Mother was another story.

I have never come to terms with the fact that my Mother failed to protect me from the physical and mental abuse my Father lavished upon us. My Mother who was Russian never quite lived up to the reputation of the overly protective Russian Mother willing to give anything, even her life in defense of her children. Perhaps it was her position in this family scenario that she would allow my Father the freedom to demonstrate the dark side of his soul. My

Mother did nothing in terms of squelching my Fathers unbridled darkness.

My Mother was an enabler.

We all have choices in life. Often times an abused and love-starved child will often emulate what the Parent taught. Perhaps with some souls the ability to love must be nurtured and taught. I believe that it is evolutionary. We are all at different levels of growth and many factors have either a positive or negative effect on the developing soul.

I decided, early in my childhood that my children and those around me would receive the love from me that I found so desperately lacking in my parents. Perhaps this was simply my nature or perhaps it was a conscious effort on my part or, maybe it was a blend of the two.

What makes an abused child in turn abuse his or her children? Is it karmic retribution? Is it a lesson that isn't yet learned? Must the abused child continue to be abused through many lives before he or she "gets it" and stops the hurt and the madness?

To the world, our family appeared happy, prosperous, perhaps even privileged, but in reality we were destitute in regards to those things that mattered most. We received no direction from our Parents.

But the synchronicity of the universe is perfect. As a family the situation we all found ourselves in was in fact a chance to learn from each other. My Mother and in particular my Father though older physically were, and are students of their offspring. It was through the guidance of their children that they had the most to learn and through learning came soul growth.

I have often wondered perhaps to excess why I was chosen to be the focus of my Father's inhumanity. I have come to numerous conclusions and I am quite certain of their divine truths. More importantly they are a source of much reassurance. I am as certain of them as I am certain of the fact that I am sitting here writing these words.

I have often been asked why I turned out to be quite the opposite of my parents. How was I able to maintain a mental and emotional balance and emerge from childhood mentally intact?

I believe the answer is a simple one. I having incarnated as my Father's child. I was sent to him for the purpose of his growth. Our family was one of design, choreographed in effect to present the best opportunity for all to advance spiritually. Stated simply, as souls we are not all on the same levels of awareness or understanding at the same time. It's not a race nor is it a competition to see who arrives at a perfected state. Growth is a process and we shall all achieve it. Sooner or later we must achieve perfection.

Many times we volunteer to be placed in uncomfortable positions for the benefit of others to aid in their growth. It is a metaphorical contract that we agree to. I can safely refer to this as a state of love and all who enter into it benefit greatly.

My Father was incapable of breaking my spirit or to be more precise I refused to revert to an emotional or spiritual state that I had grown out of eons ago. So in reality I was safe in this respect. And because I was safe I was the perfect volunteer for this particular situation.

There are no accidents in our multi-faceted existence. All is in perfect harmony in relation to itself. But for the moment I was content with the prosaic.

Mom asked me to help her start dinner and I was happy to do so hoping it would take my mind off of the day's events. We made small talk as we worked and she asked me how my day was. I told her that I had spent the day with Deana, but I did not tell her of our terrifying encounter with the old man, I knew better than that. Telling her of the encounter would only serve to open a Pandora's box of questioning and innuendo.

From the upstairs bedroom we could hear my Father calling out demanding that someone answer the phone. In those days we only had one house phone and ours was situated in the living room. With the hum of the food mixer at work neither of us heard the phone ring.

My Mother turned nervously to me and requested that I answer the phone. I ran to the living room and quickly picked up the receiver;

"Hello?" I gasped.

"This is the long distant operator will you accept a call from Seattle Washington?" the female operator on the other end inquired.

I hesitated. I thought if I accepted a long distance call not knowing who it was I could be in trouble with my Father, but if I didn't accept the call I could also get into trouble. I decided to accept the call.

"Yes I will accept," I said as I prayed my choice to accept was correct.

"Thank you go ahead" were the operator's instructions.

"Hello?"

But there was silence. In a much louder and firmer tone I repeated myself. "Hello?" I said again.

"I am coming to kill you" the voice on the other end threatened.

"What?" I screamed. I struggled to maintain my grip on the phone. I felt my knees begin to buckle and I felt I was going to faint.

Once again he repeated himself; "I am coming to kill you."

I regained control of my legs and reaffirmed my grip on the receiver.

The voice was that of an elderly man. He sounded hoarse and his words crackled as though his throat was dry with age. The connection itself appeared bad as it was full of static and strange humming noises that made it sound otherworldly. Although I cannot fully explain it I received the distinct impression that he was speaking to me from a distance, a very great distance indeed.

Dropping the phone I turned and quickly ascended the stairs to my bedroom. Slamming the door behind me must have made quite a racket.

"Who's that slamming my bloody doors?" roared my Father who was now in the hallway and making great haste toward my room.

"It's just me daddy" I said in a pleading voice.

Having reprimanded me for my indiscretion with his door he asked me who the caller was. Hesitantly I told him that it was only one of my girlfriends. Satisfied with the answer he warned me not to be late for dinner.

I found myself once again staring out of my bedroom window. I began sobbing and shaking uncontrollably. I felt as though I were the only person in the universe. The old man's words repeated over and over again in my mind like a broken record that refused to stop turning.

I was being haunted.

At six I joined my family for dinner in the kitchen. I was still distraught and barely able to eat. Unable to control myself any longer I broke into tears.

"What's the matter Kathy?" my Mother asked.

"She probably bought the wrong bloody lipstick," quipped my Father.

With my Father's remark the tears flowed like a broken water main.

In a rare moment of tenderness my Mother rose from her chair placing herself behind me. She held me tightly whispering in my ear that everything was all right.

But the tears refused to stop. Dinner had come to a standstill, as I became everyone's unwilling focal point.

My Father who was devoid of continence became increasingly agitated and screamed out to me across the table; "You will tell us what the problem is or I will put my boot up your bloody arse!"

And that was no idle threat!

My Mother seated herself and the rest of the family sat silently as I began my story. I related to them the day's events beginning with the encounter Deana and I had with the "old man". My Father sat stunned as I finished the story. Raising from his chair he pompously proclaimed; "I shall call the authorities immediately!"

Leaving the kitchen he rushed toward the direction of the phone. I glanced at my Mother only to see that she had resumed eating her meal. With obvious indifference, Cynthia too was quietly and busily picking through her plate. Both Rob and Steve displayed obvious concern and shock, but were instructed by my Mother to continue with their dinner. Obediently they both complied.

Once again I was emotionally deserted by those closest to me.

My Father re-entered the Kitchen and informed me that he spoke to the Police and that they would be sending an Officer to investigate "my little matter".

With dinner completed I was instructed to remain downstairs while the rest of the family went upstairs. I felt confident now that help was on the way. I was eager to help the Police with their investigation and to put this matter to rest. I only hoped and dreamed that the detectives they sent over were young and good looking.

Some time had passed when there came a knock at the door.

I opened the door to find one of Burlingame's best. He introduced himself as Officer Williams. If you recall Peter Falk in the series Colombo then you can imagine what he looked like, only this one was in uniform and about ninety pounds heavier.

"Don't they have physical standards for these guys" I wondered to myself.

I beckoned Officer Williams to enter. As I stood aside for him to enter I could see that his evening's dinner created a modern art masterpiece with his shirt and tie as the canvas.

I motioned for him to sit on my Fathers Easy Chair as I sat on the couch. Incredulously he looked into my eyes. Pulling his little notebook out of his shirt pocket he readied his pen as he stretched both legs out in front of him and yawned. His burgeoning stomach stretched the limits of the buttons on his shirt and I thought they must surely pop off and fly across the room.

Not quite finished with his yawn and with a cordial attempt at covering his gaping mouth with his right hand he asked for my full name.

With the perfunctory questioning at an end Officer Williams got into the meat and potatoes of the questioning by asking me to give him the full details of my "crank call". The brevity of my explanation must have even shocked Officer Williams, but I could see that I was wasting both his time and mine.

The Officer promised to make a full report and informed me that someone would get back once the "investigation" was completed.

I showed Officer Williams to the door and returned to my bedroom. My Mother and Father were readying themselves for a cocktail party and couldn't be bothered with the results of my interview with the Police.

"At least I didn't receive a beating from my Father," was the conclusion that occurred to me.

I slowly closed my eyes and struggled to clear my mind. Taking a deep breath I focused on the area centered between my eyes and slightly above. My mind began to quiet and I concentrated on the blackness. I didn't realize it at the time, but I was actually placing myself into a meditative state. It was a natural ability I had since early childhood, a form of escapism really.

As I drifted through the vastness of my consciousness I vaguely became aware of a pinpoint of light centered within my "view". The light grew closer and larger until it was discernable as the image of a person. As it came closer it slowed and came into focus. Much to my surprise I was once again face-to-face with the "Old Man". It was the same old man who made his presence known to me just before I died and the same old man who menacingly starred at me on the street today. Certainly he was also the same old man who just this evening threatened to kill me.

My soul shuddered as I braced for a renewed engagement.

But there was a seeming change in his demeanor. The formerly cruel and menacing stare was now replaced with a smiling and caring face. His eyes exuded warmth and understanding. I felt he had a message for me.

As we gazed upon each other I understood many things in an instant.

The "old man" as I called him was simply a projection of my mind. He was what many cultures refer to as "Death" or, the "Angel of Death". An archetype really. They may come in many forms and many guises as they intrude upon our consciousness. Some may wear a veil or a hood and some may even carry a scythe as they "harvest" souls. The Death Archetype may differ slightly from culture to culture and person to person. He always represents Death or to be more exact he represents change, for Death is change and should not be confused with finality because within the mind of the Universe there is no finality only a change of expression.

There was a reason that I found myself "stopped" in this particular year and even more so on this particular day. I can only assume that the old man was of significant symbolic relevance.

The "old man" who continued to smile faded from my mind as I drifted into sleep.

Once again I found myself leaving this "time" as I was projected forward into my life.

As though I were viewing a slide show scenes from my life passed quickly in front of me. Seemingly insignificant incidents involving inter-personal relationships took on new meaning. On a soul level I felt all the pain I inflicted on those who I callously belittled. I realized the result of and the life altering effect that negative words inflicted upon those close to me and those not so close to me. I understood the ramifications of all actions and the "butterfly effect" of all inactions and how I could have changed a little bit of the world had I only taken the correct action. It was all so crystal clear.

I became witness to every event in my life as it unfolded. As I grew from an adolescent young girl into a woman I comprehended the meaning and purpose of our existence.

During those years family life changed little. The sadistic beatings inflicted upon me by my Father and his incessant verbal attacks upon my self-worth continued. My Mother's apparent emotional and mental detachment from her children persisted and became only more evident.

Family members became more estranged from one another. We were a fragmented family divided into two basic camps: Father, Mother, and Cynthia occupied the hierarchy within the unit, leaving myself, Rob, and Steve in the secondary rung of the "pecking order".

But there were good times also. I was very close to both of my brothers. A bond developed during those years that still exist today. Socially these were the best years of my life. The majority of my time was spent with friends and they all wanted readings and I was happy to comply. Word spread concerning my accuracy rate and the phone rang non-stop at my house much to the chagrin of my Father.

At school I excelled. I found quite by accident that if I placed a schoolbook under my pillow at night the next morning all information from the book had been absorbed and retained. I never studied for tests as it all came almost too easy for me.

Oh yes, there was something else I found a liking for, and that was boys, but not just any old boy there was a certain type I was attracted to.

The scenes continued to rush by and once again I decided to slow things down for a closer more nostalgic look.

It occurred to me that I really enjoyed this time in my earthly life. This time was a time of new love and supreme adventure. After all I had not been stopped nor forbidden from "stopping" the last time. So in affect I was the captain of the ship, the navigator of my own destiny.

In life, free will and self-determination has always been of capital importance to me. So why would it be any different in the spirit plane? I was free to do as I pleased and for the moment it pleased me to fully relive this time.

But what have I done for Humanity? This was a question that continued to dance in my thoughts.

What have I done for Humanity?

CHAPTER FIVE

The Honeymoon Begins

My insistence catapulted me back into the flesh. Finding myself once again back in my bedroom and encased in a physical body was quite shocking. The room spun. I reached out with both hands and grasped at my bedspread in an attempt to ground myself.

This time the return wasn't quite as easy. I struggled to my feet as I held on to the bed. Like a drunken sailor with my head still spinning I made my way to my closet door. Still hanging like an old friend was the three quarter length mirror. I focused on my image as the spinning sensation began to dissipate.

The reflection in that mirror was of me at the age of seventeen.

"My what a difference a few years make," I laughingly thought as I examined my expanded bust line.

"I think I'm going to like this," I whispered to myself.

Just then the phone rang. Immediately, I lunged for the receiver. "Hello?" I asked.

"Well hello" It was Larry. Larry was my current fling and although unknown to me at the time, he would be the man I would marry.

Plans were made for the evening and Larry told me he would be by at about six that evening to pick me up.

I met Larry at school. I was fifteen and Larry was seventeen. He was from the "wrong side of the tracks," as my Father liked to call it, but that was what I liked about him. I liked the bad boys, and Larry was a bad boy.

Like my Father, Larry was of Portuguese descent. Of diminutive height, Larry compensated this perceived inadequacy with an obsessive pursuit of bodybuilding. Larry bulged with overly ripe muscles always sure to show them off with tight fitting shirts even tighter fitting jeans and the ever-present black leather vest.

But Larry's physical presence was only part of his mystique because it fit in so perfectly with the tough crowd he ran with. Everyone knew that Larry and his friends were heavily into drugs. Everyone also knew that if you needed drugs Larry's friends could get it for you no matter what it was.

The respect attributed to Larry and his gang was born of fear and there was good reason to fear this group because they were capable of anything. Everyone knew this. It was perhaps this same fear that elicited the opposite reaction in me as it drove me precariously closer to him.

But I too was typecast. The girls I hung out with were referred to as the "rich bitches". In actuality we were a loosely knit group of young girls whose families lived in the Burlingame Hills section of the peninsula. The human psyche has a need to classify everything.

It was 1973 and hip huggers were in fashion. Needless to say we took full advantage of the style. The lower the better was our motto when it came to our jeans. Hip huggers and halter tops were the uniform of the day and our marching orders were to make as many young males swoon with desire as we slowly and deliberately strode by.

With certainty however our reputations were not deserved. Albeit we were not considered "loose" girls since I and the majority of my friends were still virtuous. Naturally there was the occasional puff of a Marijuana joint, but this was about as far as it went. All in all we were actually a very wholesome group with many of us spending most of our time with sports or similarly healthy pursuits. When you play with fire however often times there is a chance you may get burnt. So on the last day of school and on a bet from one of the girls in my group we decided we would stride past Larry and his friends.

It was a beautifully hot day and from somewhere in the distance a radio played "California Girls" by the Beach Boys. How fitting I thought as we began our slow methodical approach toward this den of wolves. Larry and his group normally occupied this area during lunch and sure enough, there they were.

Today would be different in many ways. Today would be one of those days where one through the most minor of decisions alters the course of her existence enabling a domino effect of circumstances to take place.

Always alert, Larry who was busily huddled with five of his friends barely even noticed us as we walked ever closer. Rightly so, for it was the Police that Larry's group was worried about. If

Larry and company weren't smoking weed then they were most assuredly selling it. We presented no threat, and besides they were too busy getting high to even notice, or so we thought. After all, I knew what the end result was. I had been through this once before. I knew what was going to happen before it happened. But it didn't matter. I had chosen to slow this down and look at the entire situation from a different perspective.

The sweet smell of Marijuana drifted through the air and became stronger as we grew closer to Larry and his friends.

I was waiting for the magic moment that I knew was coming.

And come it did. As we strolled by Larry looked up and locked his eyes with mine. Stepping forward he uttered those words that would mark the beginning of seven tempestuous years.

"Hi I'm Larry. Who are you I've seen you around?"

Larry and I conversed briefly, but I wasn't to see him again for quite a few months when quite by accident we both attended a party at a friend's house. Larry asked me out the following weekend. And so it began.

The months flew by and my relationship with Larry grew ever stronger. But Larry was my secret. My parents knew I was seeing someone but they didn't know how serious I was about him nor did they know who he was.

It was a terrible morass. I was with a man who I thought I was completely in love with, but unable to introduce to my family.

I maintained my "real time" reliving of this part of my life. I didn't know why at the time I just knew that there was a reason for doing so. Somewhere deep inside me I knew that this portion of my life had to be more closely analyzed. Every emotion and every word spoken by me or said to me was felt on a level I never knew possible. Every ramification involved in every second of life now made sense to me. But it was this phase of my life that I somehow knew was very important in the understanding of self and the condition that I now found myself in, one that would affect the course of my life and future lives.

Time passed swiftly and many lessons were not only relived but for the first time they were understood and felt at soul level.

Free will no longer applied to me. I was fully engulfed in a replay of my life and although I felt I was freely making decisions in fact I was not. All of my actions were fully automated and complete. It was not up to me to change the course of life through independent action because I was merely an observer. If I anticipated an event and felt I could change the outcome by changing my present action I found that I was incapable of doing so. I was not free to change any of the outcomes, but to only re-experience them, learn from them, and to feel them.

I continued to keep Larry my secret, but only to my parents. My friends were a different story. I wanted to show Larry off to them. It didn't matter to me that he was taking what we called "heavy duty drugs." After all he was much older than I and it was the 70's. At the time it seemed everyone was doing drugs.

Deep inside though I knew that the heavy amounts of drugs Larry ingested wasn't comparable to what the average young person of that era experimented with or periodically tried. Larry was only a couple of steps away from being a full-blown addict. I understood this but I pushed it to the back of my mind. I marginalized its effect on Larry and its effect on our relationship.

About two years passed and Larry and I became more involved. I guess you could say that the wild courtship had cooled somewhat. We dated on weekends and saw each other as much as we could during the week. Larry had a menial job at a small paint shop in Burlingame. It didn't pay much, but it allowed Larry to live independently. It also sustained his drug use.

It was at this point in our relationship that I felt my Father be damned I will introduce Larry to my Parents.

It was Friday night and as usual Larry called with plans for the evening, but on this evening instead of meeting Larry somewhere other than my house I told him to pick me up at my home. Reluctantly Larry agreed.

Naturally Larry was well aware of my relationship with my parents and especially my Father. He was also aware of my Father's violent temper and propensity to physically abuse me when it suited his mood. Larry often remarked that it was because my Father was full blood Portuguese. But so was Larry. So on a fine summer's night in 1976 Larry arrived at my house. My entire family was present. I told no one that Larry would be picking me up.

"Get the bloody door" came the cry from my Father.

"I will get it daddy," I yelled out as I almost flew down the stairs toward the front door. I opened it and immediately saw that Larry was higher than a kite. With bloodshot eyes and a glazed stare Larry looked like he was having difficulty simply standing there.

Needless to say I was shocked and very disappointed not only with the fact that he was high, but he was dressed like a street thug, which of course was his typical dress.

"I thought you were going to wear something nice," I angrily whispered.

Dressed in his usual fashion Larry was a sight to behold. Larry sported his usual dirty white t-shirt, black well-worn vest, jeans and black motorcycle boots. I trembled at the idea of introducing him to my Father.

I took Larry by the hand and led him toward the kitchen where my parents were just finishing up Dinner. Surprisingly my first introduction of Larry to my parents went very well. Larry was very polite and respectful and my parents were quite cordial and accepting. Perhaps it was the fact that my Father sensed that he would soon be rid of me that tempered his response to Larry.

Larry's first meeting with my parents ended abruptly when my Father without word proceeded to his bedroom slamming the door behind him.

The introduction was a success! Although anyone would interpret Father's behavior as crass and rude it was actually quite civilized based on my Father's standards and normal inter action with others.

Saying our goodbyes to my Mother, Larry and I left for Larry's parents' home. We were both invited for Dinner and Larry was expecting quite a large gathering of relatives. It was while driving to his parent's home and after lighting up a joint of Marijuana that Larry proposed to me. It came as no surprise to me. Of course I was expecting it. I knew it was coming.

It wasn't a very romantic proposal, but then again what did I know about proposals? I accepted of course. I would do anything to leave my Father's house and after all I was in love with Larry.

As Larry drove I starred out the window at the gathering fog on the San Bruno mountains. The smell of Marijuana danced upon my nostrils and I felt content. I imagined a time free of physical and mental abuse, a time spent with a man who cared about me, a man who would never cause me any harm, a man who would protect me from the pain of the world, a man who could protect me from my Father. I was filled with unspeakable anticipation.

We arrived at Larry's Fathers to find the house filled with his relatives. Larry enjoyed a close-knit family and large gatherings for dinner and other occasions were traditional. I enjoyed Larry's family and got along especially well with his Mother Donna. Donna was a very nurturing and loving Mother to all of her children. I found her quite the opposite of my Mother and because of this I was strongly attracted to her.

I felt very lucky indeed.

It was during Dinner that Larry announced to his family that we were engaged. Larry raised his beer bottle from the table and shouted; "Hey everybody listen up." His announcement fell on deaf ears, as the chatter around the table continued.

Once again he exclaimed; "Hey God damn it listen up. I got an announcement."

This time the table fell gradually silent as Larry proclaimed our engagement. They all simply stared blankly only for a moment and then went back to eating their dinners. Donna was the only one who showed any emotion as she quickly stood from her chair and rushed over to hug me.

"Congratulations Kathy," she said as she hugged me tightly. Tears began to stream from her eyes. Sitting back down as quickly as she rose she continued with her Dinner.

The rest of the evening's topic was that of the upcoming football game between the 49ers and the Packers. Not another word of our engagement was spoken. Quietly I finished my dinner. We said our goodbyes and departed.

I suppose I was expecting more fanfare, after all it isn't every day that you get engaged. The fog from the ocean filled the streets as we drove toward our next stop.

Looking through the fog once again I began to reflect on my present set of circumstances. I thought that I loved Larry, but I was also desperate to leave my Father's house.

Then the following thoughts struck me like a lightning bolt from the heavens.

"It came to pass. It did not come to stay, and it only came to pass."

History has proven this to be a very true statement. Everything that ever was has passed. One day we too will pass. It is important for us to remember that truth during these so-called turbulent times, which are no more or less turbulent than times past. The one thought that has always helped me get through was knowing it would not last forever. This too shall pass. Another phrase that helps me daily is "going through it." People use this phrase all the time. I'm going through this or I'm going through that. The answer is inherent within this phrase. Keep going through it and do not stop. Focus on answers and solutions. When you are going through hell don't stop and take a picture. You will only experience this one-day at a time. There are no promises that life will be easy. Years ago I decided that life is never really what it seems, it's always more.

Larry pulled to the curb and shut off the engine. This was his best friend's house and the party was already raging. Hard rock music and whoops of laughter as well as screams of intoxication mixed with music filled the air.

It would be another night of the same old thing, the drinking, the drug use, and unlike Larry I grew bored of its repetition.

Larry and the majority of his friends were committed drug users and alcoholics. Years later the majority of them would pay the price for their debauchery. Many would die at an early age either by drugs or alcoholism. Others became permanent rotting figures at neighborhood bars waiting their turn.

A few months later Larry and I were married. It was a traditional Catholic wedding. In addition to my family and Larry's there were seventy-five people in attendance. It was quite a pleasant affair actually and I had hoped it would be a portent of things to come.

Our reception was held at a very old Italian restaurant in Burlingame. Even my Father got drunk, so drunk that he gave me a hug and wished me luck. With everyone thoroughly awash in alcohol the reception broke up about 9:00 PM. With rice raining upon us Larry and I departed the restaurant to begin our honeymoon.

It was a three hour drive to Carmel. Arriving around midnight we checked into a small but quaint Hotel near the Monterey Bay. We were both very tired and no sooner did Larry "try out" the bed then he was snoring. I inspected the room and then seated myself on the small chair by a table near the front door. My gaze turned to Larry who, still in his tuxedo snored even louder.

It became fully apparent to me at that moment that I had made a mistake in marrying him. I entertained many fantasies during the preceding months. It appeared that the honeymoon was over before it ever began. It was all so anti-climatic.

I rose from the chair and changed into my pajamas while settling in next to Larry. The steady drone of his snoring eventually put me to sleep. Sleep was something I certainly welcomed. Sleep was a friend and a welcomed escape mechanism from my life. Our honeymoon was scheduled to end that Sunday night as both of us had to be back to work Monday morning.

The next two days with Larry was unbearable. From the moment we woke until the time we went to sleep we fought. We fought about nothing and we fought about everything. We fought more during those two days in Carmel than in the combined prior three years of our relationship and it would only get worse.

Sunday night we drove back to Burlingame. There was no fighting and there was no talking.

In retrospect I must admit that much of the fighting was initiated by me. I made a mistake in marrying Larry and the realization of this mistake was beginning to manifest in my treatment toward him. We arrived at our apartment and you could cut the raw hostile atmosphere with a knife. Larry who had been diagnosed two years earlier with diabetes was in the process of administering insulin shots. The Doctor told him that one of the possible contributing factors for its onset was the voluminous amount of drugs Larry had ingested over the years. Larry discounted this assumption however and put the blame elsewhere. Certainly it was multiple contributing factors, which naturally included heredity, as diabetes did run in his family.

How old he looked as I watched him insert the needle. Rising slowly from his chair Larry changed into pajamas and without word went to bed. The next day we both arose early to go our respective jobs. Larry was a box assembler at a nearby plant and I looked forward to returning to my job as a medical assistant at a local GYN Clinic. Larry left the Apartment first. He softly and tenderly kissed me goodbye.

The thought passed through my mind that perhaps getting back into our normal routine of working might bring our relationship back to normalcy. That day I got off work and I decided that a wonderful dinner would perhaps smooth things out with Larry. The way to a man's heart as my Mother taught me was through his stomach. There was an upscale specialty store nearby and although we were short on funds I spent the money and picked up a sirloin roast, broccoli, and potatoes. This would be our first official dinner at home and I knew that roast beef was Larry's favorite.

The smell of the roast slowly began to permeate the apartment as I hurriedly began the side dishes. I felt exhilarated and happy in anticipation of Larry's arrival. I had just finished setting the dinner table when I heard the sound of Larry opening the front door.

I rushed to greet him. I threw both arms around him and asked him how his day was.

"Wonderful just wonderful" he said coldly. He starred at me briefly then slowly pushing me away he turned and walked to the couch seating himself. Grabbing the television remote control from coffee table Larry fell back into the couch, stretched his legs out in front of him, and turned on the TV. Letting out a very loud and very long belch was the icing on the cake.

The excitement I felt earlier drained from me as though someone turned on a spigot within my body. Like a wounded animal looking for forgiveness I knelt down beside him placing my arm around his shoulder.

"Dinner is ready sweetheart," I said softly.

Larry turned off the television and began to rise from his chair. With a blank stare and emotionless eyes he walked toward the kitchen table and seated himself all the time completely ignoring my presence.

A wave of cold energy struck me like an unseen tidal wave. I struggled to compose myself. I busied myself placing the dinner on the table as Larry who appearing comatose-like continued staring at his plate. With all of the food placed on the table I began cutting the meat placing the largest most desirable piece on Larry's plate.

Larry from his seated position and without warning backhanded me with a strike flush on my right temple. The strike was completely unexpected and I never even saw it coming.

The next thing I recall is seeing a flash of light. I felt myself being hurled backwards like a rag doll. Strangely there was no pain, not at that point at least. Everything slowed down. All of my senses were on half speed.

I landed flat on my back in the living room. I was dazed and not knowing where I was I looked up from the floor only to see Larry coming for me. He looked like a crazed monster. I couldn't believe he had struck me. I covered my face and prepared myself for the next strike, but instead of hitting me Larry who was now down on his hands and knees pulled me from the ground and held me close. Sobbing uncontrollably he begged for my forgiveness promising me that it would never happen again.

I spent the remainder of that evening in total shock and utter bewilderment. I was still bleeding from the right temple and was physically disoriented, but not disoriented enough to not realize that I had left one monster for another, one impossible position for another intolerable prison.

Many thoughts crossed my mind that night. I rationalized that Larry was diabetic, and I knew from my medical background that many of the medications that diabetics took could play havoc with their emotions and psyche in general. Perhaps I was no good, as my Father would remind me almost every day of my life. I felt totally isolated from the world. I wanted to call a friend. I certainly had many, but this wasn't something I was willing to share with anyone, at least not yet.

I concluded that the problem between Larry and I was repairable. Perhaps he could change medications. Just maybe I could change somehow and that would make Larry happy. After all we were newlyweds and I knew that Larry loved me. I became confident again, my life with Larry would be wonderful and I would see to it.

As the weeks and months went by Larry and I continued to grow farther and farther apart. The beatings and verbal abuse continued and to tell you the truth I almost became accustomed to it, in the same fashion that I became accustomed to my Father's abuse. Larry was merely an extension of the horror.

Our lives went on and every day was exactly like the last one. The hum-drum existence was punctuated at least weekly by Larry becoming enraged and then taking his anger out on me with various degrees of physical abuse.

The fantasy I so optimistically entertained of our union becoming wonderful was just that, a fantasy. All stories must have an end and all cycles end also. My particular cycle came to its final crescendo on a very cold and windy November night when I found myself once again preparing Dinner for a man who I now found myself despising.

"I want my Dinner now" he said, slamming the front door behind him. I ignored his demand and continued placing the plates on the table. The next thing I was aware of was being grabbed from behind and spun around. The last thing I remember seeing was Larry's enraged face.

Slowly and with great pain I opened my eyes. My ears were ringing and the pain in the back of my neck was immense. I was staring at the ceiling of the kitchen. I realized I was flat on my back. Larry had knocked me unconscious. I wondered how long I had been lying there. I wondered if Larry was still there.

"Larry help me," I uttered from my now prone position.

"Larry help me," I said once again only this time louder.

There was no reply. With all of my strength I managed to turn over on my left side. I looked to the wall clock and saw that it said 7:30. Larry got home at 7:00 o'clock. I had been unconscious for almost half an hour. A few more minutes passed and I mustered the strength to get up. I looked for Larry, but he wasn't in the apartment.

I began crying hysterically and decided that I would have to call someone. I could no longer keep this nightmare to myself. I needed help or he would kill me.

I decided to call Marie. Marie was a close friend and if I could talk to anyone who would understand it would be her. I attempted to calm myself by taking in long deep breaths. The room spun ever so slightly as I reached for the phone.

Thankfully Marie was home. Hysterically I spilled my guts to her in one breath.

"Kathy you have to get out of there now" Marie said in a low and muffled voice.

Marie instructed me to stay by the phone and to watch the door. She would call back in a minute, but first she needed to make a call. She told me that if Larry came back I was to bolt for the door and run for my life. Reassuring me I would be all right she hung up.

Pensively I placed the phone on the receiver. My stare became transfixed on the front door. My left hand remained clamped on the phones receiver. I didn't move, nor did I even dare blink.

What felt like an eternity passed when the phone rang.

"Hello" I said.

It was Marie. "Get your ass over to my apartment as fast as you can you are staying with us,"

"I'm on my way" was my hurried reply.

I dropped the phone to the floor and ran to the bedroom. Retrieving my suitcase from the closet I began packing it with clothing. Jeans, dresses, shoes, all were thrown into the suitcase from various spots within the room.

My next stop was the bathroom. Hairdryer, combs and brushes, tooth brush and toothpaste, all items landed on top of the clothing within the suitcase.

Satisfied that I had all the items needed I fell upon the pile of clothing compressing them within the case. With almost superhuman strength born of desperation I closed and locked the suitcase.

With suitcase in hand I made a mad dash for the front door. My heart raced with fear that I would encounter Larry at the front door or in the hallway of the Apartment Complex.

Fate was with me. I wasted no time in my retreat from hell. In an instant I found myself on the street and literally running toward Marie's apartment that thankfully was only blocks away.

Before I could knock twice Marie flung the door open and grabbing me by the arm pulled me into the safety of her apartment. She quickly closed and double locked the door. We stared at each other for a moment and then quickly embraced. Marie stroked the back of my head and whispered reassuring words to me. Pushing me away she starred compassionately into my eyes.

"Kathy you are going to Modesto. My mom and dad said you can stay with them for a while, but in the mean time we got to clean up your face" she said. "Just look at you Kathy how many times did he punch you"

"I don't know," I said. I didn't want to think about. I only wished to forget it. I knew that it was the last time it would happen and I only wished for it to fade into memory.

The next morning Marie drove me the 100 miles to Modesto. Modesto is a small mostly agricultural town east of San Francisco. It was a good place to hide out. Marie's parents were wonderful people and always treated me like I was their daughter. I would enjoy my rest bit there.

My stay in Modesto was a mere five days. But it gave me ample time to reflect on my life up to this point. I understood that my life was about to take a drastic change. I came to grips with the little choices I made that had big effects on every aspect of my life. Naturally I hadn't chosen to be born of my Parents, born of a Father who was sadistically brutal to me. Or did I make that choice? At a certain point in time and space did I make the choice to come into a family where my lessons would be tough and traumatic? Perhaps a karmic balancing act was in play. Naturally I made the choice to marry Larry, but certainly at the time I had no idea that he would become a younger version of my Father, and just as brutal in his senseless rages.

CHAPTER SIX

A New Man

Though the time I spent in Modesto was in fact healing I knew it was time to leave. I was young and had my whole life ahead of me. I was in constant contact with my Mother and the more we talked the more she convinced me I must come home. But what of my Father, what were his views on welcoming me back into his home? After all he couldn't wait for me to leave. My Father never experienced the "empty nest" syndrome; in fact I doubt that he ever heard of it.

Marie dropped me off at my parents that evening. My Mother was there at the front door waiting for me and as I ascended the stairs she quickly rushed forward and embraced me tightly. I cried at that moment and the tears wouldn't stop.

As we turned and entered the house I felt a great sense of relief. "Where's dad?" I asked.

"Oh, he was tired and turned in early. You know he works very hard," she said apologetically.

That night mother and I sat sipping tea in the kitchen. I spilled out my heart to her and all that had happened. All those things I had kept hidden from her concerning Larry I now revealed.

Incredulously she only stared at me in obvious disbelief.

"Why didn't you tell us about this before Kathy?" she said.

"You don't believe me?"

"It's not that I don't believe you, but I just couldn't imagine Larry doing this to you, the two of you seemed to have such a good relationship."

We talked for another hour, and my Mother's tone didn't change. We both turned in and in the morning I awoke to my Father calling me down to the kitchen.

Entering the kitchen I was met by my Father who curtly informed me that I had one month to "get my act together" and get out.

My Mother stood by the sink quietly drinking her cup of coffee as my Father without further ado rushed from the kitchen and out the door as he headed for work.

"Your Father thinks you should have tried a little harder to make it work with Larry you know" she said softly, but sternly.

I turned and began to walk from the kitchen.

"I will be out in a month," I said as I pushed the kitchen door open.

I quickly dressed for work and looked forward to returning to my Job. The Medical Center had been extremely understanding and supportive for allowing me time off.

I was desperate now and had to formulate a plan. All of the money Larry and I saved was in the Bank. It was a large sum of money especially in those days and certainly for two struggling young persons to save $17.000.00 dollars was quite a feat.

Lunchtime arrived and I quickly left the office almost running to the Bank. I handed the prewritten check written to cash to the teller in the amount of $8.500 dollars. The amount was my half of the savings.

The teller looked pensively into the computer only to tell me:

"I'm sorry but this account has been closed out"

My head began to spin.

"Closed out when?" I screamed hysterically.

"It was closed out on the 17th of this month" she replied. Larry closed out the account and with it thousands of dollars of the money I helped to contribute.

I was penniless. With $5.00 left to my name I felt I had been hit by lightning. I walked away slowly, sheepishly, I felt beaten. I reluctantly resigned myself to the fact that I had been completely dominated both physically and financially by a reprobate who I never would have had anything to do with had I not been desperate to leave my Fathers house. My friends at the time warned that he was beneath me and that I would suffer in the end. They were right.

During my walk back to work I prayed very deeply. I loved God and I knew he loved me. He would not forsake me, but I knew I would need to put forth the effort also.

When I arrived back at work I sat down at my desk, took out a notepad and pen and began working out the figures. My Father gave me one month and one month equated to two paychecks, if I watched every penny I could afford a small and Spartan studio apartment.

The desperation I had felt drained from my body and I began to relax. The rest of the day at work went well. I had a plan and I would not fail myself.

The month flew by and much to my Father's delight I was able to rent a small but very cute apartment in the Burlingame area. Moving in was a breeze because I had no furniture to move in save for a mattress that Marie had no use for and happily donated to me. First, last, and a small deposit completely depleted my Bank account leaving me with about $25.00 to see me through the following two weeks. Broke but elated as I began my new life I surveyed my new apartment and took mental note as to how I would decorate it. It was small and empty, but it was mine.

The following month I began a process through the Catholic Church requesting an annulment of my marriage with Larry. I was told that if it were approved it could take up to six months to go through and may have to be approved by the Bishop.

The weeks and months went by and my life began to stabilize. I was told by two of my girlfriends that Larry had contacted them with regard to my whereabouts. Everyone I knew was instructed to keep secret my whereabouts. And then one day while at work I was told that my husband was at the front desk demanding to see me. In a panic I raced down the hallway. Jill the receptionist at the front desk had apparently lost her temper with Larry and dialed 911. Jill and I were great friends and she wasn't the type who would easily be intimidated by Larry. Realizing whom Jill had just called Larry left in a hurry. The last thing Larry wanted was to go to jail. It was the one thing that terrified him most.

The cat and mouse game with Larry continued for a few more months. I became an expert at counter-espionage tactics sometimes leaving work early and sometimes late, always looking over my shoulder taking different routes home each time. After a while, it appeared that Larry was beginning to lose interest in me.

The Catholic Church finally granted my annulment from Larry. It was over and I was glad.

The next few months caught me still looking over my shoulder, but my life became calm and the repetition of the work-a-day world was therapeutic.

My apartment began to come together also. I furnished it slowly buying only those furnishings of quality and functionality. If there was but one thing my Father taught us all it was to buy only the best, not only in clothes but in furnishings as well. His logic was correct of course in that costlier items were of better quality and simply lasted longer.

I also began to date other men. Slowly, methodically, and I must admit with great care I approached the dating scene once again, but only with great trepidation and uncertainty.

Any man who asked me out was suspect. Most dates were one-time affairs. I no longer trusted men. I feared that the next man who I allowed to come close would only feign kindness and eventually turn on me like a Rattlesnake.

But on this particular Friday night little did I know that my life was about to make another major course correction.

The phone rang and it was my girlfriend Diana.

Diana and I agreed to meet at our local watering hole on Burlingame Avenue.

Somehow I must have known instinctively to look my best. For the first time in a long time I spent almost two hours getting ready that night. With what felt like electricity in the air my anticipation of the night grew with every passing second.

Finally with my hair perfect, makeup perhaps a bit overdone I put the finishing touches on with the tightest jeans in my wardrobe and a matching Top.

It was almost nine and the bar was already very busy. I pushed my way through the crowds that now lined both aisles of the club. I knew everyone there. It took an eternity to say my hellos as I slowly walked and paused my way to Deana who was engaged in conversation with Bob who was a mutual friend. He was seated at the bar and undergoing questioning by Deana. Bob was already sloshed, but so were the majority of the people in the bar. Unfortunately Alcohol and Drugs had ruined the lives of most of my friends.

Nestled between upscale boutiques on a very busy boulevard the Club was more than a place to drink, it was a rendezvous for old friends and acquaintances. Diana especially loved it because it represented to her a gold mine of information that most of us refer to as gratuitous gossip.

"Hi Deana. Hi Bob," I said with a sigh of relief.

"Hi Kathy" said Bob.

Bob grabbed me by the hand and pulled me close to him.

"Kathy I have someone I want to introduce you to. Kathy this is my buddy Mark."

"Hello Mark" I said as I offered my hand.

"Please call me Mark. I'm happy to meet you Kathy!" he said meekly.

I can't say that I looked into his eyes and knew instantly that I was going to marry Mark, but I can say that a certain feeling seemed to overwhelm me. As I have explained before it has always been difficult for me to read for myself and this just happened to be one of those times.

Mark and I sat for the rest of the night getting to know each other. Rather tall and slim and possessing dark hair and eyes Mark was of Guatemalan and Romanian descent.

Mark told me that he had just graduated from San Francisco State College with a BS in Biology. His original intent was to have become a dentist, but having lost interest in that idea he took a job with a Bay Area Bio-Chemical company where each day he dawned a special suit and used robotic arms behind a protective wall as he worked with radioactive materials.

"Real exciting " I thought, as Mark continued to describe in monotonous detail his day-to-day machinations.

But there was something on a subconscious level that intrigued me or rather, attracted me to Mark. On a gut level I felt safe with him. There was something about him that exuded a non-violent energy. I knew that on a physical level I was completely safe with him. This appealed to me. This more than anything else at this point in my life attracted me to him.

It was almost two in the morning and the Bartender had already called for last rounds. Mark offered me a ride home and I accepted. Deana and Bob were still engaged in conversation as we said our farewells to them.

I directed Marc to my apartment and he pulled his car to a stop in front of my door.

Mark turned and looked me squarely in the eyes.

"I hear you are psychic?"

"Who told you that?" I asked.

"Deana. She said you are the best."

"Well, I don't know about that, but I do sometimes even scare myself."

I placed my left hand on his right arm and looked him in the eyes.

"I can tell you this much and this I see very clearly. You will be married at a young age and you will have two daughters."

"Really?" he countered.

"Yes really and I can tell you that I see this as clearly as I am looking at you right now."

Mark turned and looked out the window.

"Can I have your number?" he asked.

"Yes I will write it down for you."

I handed him my phone number. Mark did not attempt to kiss me nor did he attempt to invite himself up to my apartment. This I liked and I was impressed.

Mark promised to call as he drove off.

I slept soundly that night knowing that a turning point or waypoint in my life had been reached. I didn't know exactly what it all meant, but on a soul level I knew something very important had just occurred.

It was a funny thing, but the longer I stayed in this "real time" life review the harder it was to see what was about to happen. Those hours with Mark were one of those segments of my life where I can say I didn't know what was going to happen next.

The weeks passed and Mark and I began to see each quite frequently. It was during this time that we became physically intimate and Mark began to spend some nights sleeping over at my apartment.

Mark and I became accustomed to each other over the next few months as most couples do. The difference between ourselves and most other couples is that we never ever argued, at least Mark didn't argue. I argued and sometimes attempted to argue, but Mark would not argue back. Mark never raised his voice, never made threatening remarks or gestures, and always either agreed with me or in a very low tone disagreed and refused to discuss the matter further. This method of discussion of course took the wind right out of my sails. There was no use in attempting an argument with Mark because it was always remained one sided!

I must admit I found it peculiar but refreshing. With Larry of course I lost every argument because inevitably all arguments turned physical and Larry always won through shear brute force.

As our relationship continued I found myself becoming very close with Marks Mother and Father. Marks Mother Janet was a wonderfully determined woman. Short in stature, but with the determination of a giant Janet arrived in this Country after World War II. Of Romanian descent, Janet survived the turmoil of war to find herself on the shores of the United States. She quickly learned the English language and began working at any job she could find, finally settling into a career as a hairdresser where she remained for many decades. Frugal from years of deprivation during the war, Janet knew how to save money. She quickly became not only my surrogate Mother, but she also became my counselor and instructor in the art of pragmatism.

I also came to love Marks Father Victorio who hailed from Guatemala. Victorio arrived in this country while in his early forties finding a job at a meat packing plant in San Francisco. Victorio was a sausage maker and was now retired. Sporting a thick shank of black hair Victorio loved to dance and at times drank to excess.

Victorio and Janet met at a Dance Party in San Francisco and wed only months later. Mark came along a little later and being an only child he was much dotted upon by his mother.

Sunday night dinners with Victorio and Janet became a tradition as the four of us very much enjoyed each other's company.

I felt as though I had finally found the Mother and the Father I had longed for all my life. The two made me feel loved, respected, important, something my own parents never made me feel.

And so it came to be on a cold December's night at a very posh San Francisco restaurant Marc graciously and romantically proposed marriage.

Our engagement came as no surprise to Marc's parents and they enthusiastically welcomed me into the family. The wedding was scheduled for the month of March the following year. Janet appointed herself coordinator and quickly set about planning the entire wedding.

The wedding took place on Saturday afternoon at St. Roberts Catholic Church in San Bruno, California. In attendance were one hundred and forty friends, relatives, and even a few people who no one recognized. During the wedding vows the Priest accidentally spit in my eye. I took this as an omen at the time. The same Priest years later was arrested in San Francisco for multiple criminal charges including embezzlement of church funds.

Naturally both my parents were also in attendance. Both were quite amiable and supportive, after all my Father had a stake in this marriage paying for one third of the costs.

The reception was held at our favorite Italian restaurant where the food was beyond description and the alcohol flowed all night. All in all the day couldn't have gone better. I felt we were off to a promising future.

The following morning we were up early and anxious to catch our flight to Maui. We booked in at a wonderful Hotel near the beach and spent a full week basking in the warm Island sun.

Our brief stay on Maui went much too quickly, but there was much to do at home. We rented a one-bedroom apartment in Millbrae right across the street from my old High School. We returned to our respective jobs and spent the next few weeks decorating our new apartment.

Mark quit his job with the Bio-chemical company and was hired on with a large Potato Chip company. He was assigned a truck route where he delivered to all the major stores. At the time I thought he was crazy for doing it, but it did pay about the same as the chemical company. Naturally I felt that with a four-year degree Mark could do much better. This was a logical assumption, but I would find that common logic had very little to do with the way Mark operated.

Mark of course had higher aspirations. He asked one morning if I knew why he quit the Chemical Company. When I told him I wasn't sure he informed me that it was apparent that I really didn't know him well.

I couldn't wait to hear this one!

"You see Kathy, I just can't bare to be locked up in an office, I need a little adventure in my life" he said.

"Adventure? Driving a Potato Chip truck is adventurous?"

"It's not just that. There is something I have always wanted to do and I have made up my mind that I'm going to do it"

"And what is that?" I queried.

"I'm going to be a cop. And not just any cop, I'm going to join the San Francisco Police Department."

"You do that and I will divorce you". I responded.

I quickly got up from the table and without another word I grabbed my coat from the closet and quickly left the apartment slamming the door behind me as a final statement.

"He wants to be a cop?" Over my dead body I thought!

I had this image in my mind when it came to cops. I viewed cops as nothing more than lazy womanizers, bullies, drunkards, doughnut thieves, and blue-collar egocentric simpletons. These are certainly brash statements, but I must admit this is what I truly thought at the time.

But I also reasoned that perhaps it would be a step up from driving a potato chip truck.

Or was it a step down?

I arrived at work minutes later in a foul mood. The man who I just married, the man who at one time aspired to become a dentist was now driving a potato chip truck and had dreams of becoming a cop!

The months marched by and we settled into our routines as all couples do. The honeymoon however was over. Reality began to set in. I must admit however that my newfound reality was a much kinder and gentler one.

Mark and I talked about buying a house and on one Sunday we decided to take a look at open houses. By the end of the day we went from casual browsers to fully dedicated buyers. There were multiple cities and neighborhoods to choose from on the San Francisco Peninsula and we explored them all.

There were two things that Mark and I wanted most at this point in our lives. One of our dreams was our very own house and the other was a child we both could love and cherish.

So when September came and went and I experienced no menstrual period I was barely able to contain myself. A home pregnancy test confirmed what I knew deep within. As a nurse I also knew that I must schedule a doctor's visit for true confirmation. I said nothing to Mark until I heard from the Doctor.

Two days later I received the call while at work. My greatest joy was realized.

That night when Mark arrived home I recall running to him and jumping in his arms. The flood of tears and overwhelming emotion were so great that I could barely utter the words.

"We are pregnant" I finally managed to tell him.

Mark gripped me tight and spun me around the room. We both began to sing and dance in an outpouring of bliss and joy that neither he nor I had ever experienced before.

My life was perfect.

On the fifth month of my pregnancy I had an ultra sound performed. It was confirmed; Mark and I were going to have a baby girl.

The following week Mark and I located a house in the San Bruno area. It was situated in nice quiet neighborhood with good schools. It had three bedrooms and two baths and it would be perfect for our now growing family.

Marks Mother and Father promised to contribute the majority of a down payment. We decided to make an offer on the house.

It felt as though the good news wouldn't stop flowing. In perfect synchronicity Mark received a call from a National Ice Cream Company. The Company liked his resume and offered him a position in sales. The position paid a substantial amount more than his present job. Certainly we needed the money and the call couldn't have come at a better time. The same week we received a call from our realtor, the offer was accepted and pending a home inspection we could move in thirty days later.

This was cause for celebration. Our lives were right on track and there was no looking back. We had our whole lives in front of us and there was no doubt that it would be wonderful.

The move went well and we settled in. I spent the better part of my free time emptying boxes, putting up pictures, and finding the perfect odds and ends for our new house.

We had been settled in perhaps two weeks when one night after falling asleep we were abruptly awakened at three in the morning. Loud crashing noises were coming from the garage area. We both darted out of bed and ran to the doorway near the steps that led to the garage.

The crashing noises abruptly stopped. What we heard next could have been taken out of the script of a "B" rated horror movie.

Standing almost breathless near the door that leads down to the garage we could hear the sounds of chains being dragged on the cement floor.

"What could that be?" I whispered.

"Maybe its Raccoons". Said Mark.

A sudden chill engulfed my body as the sounds continued. Mark slowly opened the door and peered down the darkened steps. The noises ceased.

"I'm going to call the police," Mark said as he quickly closed and locked the door.

"It won't do us any good," I warned.

I took Mark by the hand and led him back toward the bedroom. I was still deeply cold and had to wrap myself in blankets as I sat at the edge of the bed trembling.

"It wasn't a burglar, and it isn't raccoons" I told him.

As I sat with eyes closed, the image of an older deeply troubled man entered my mind's eye.

I explained to Mark that the spirit of this man still inhabits this house. I knew that he hadn't died here, but he was attracted to this house and decided to take up "residency" here.

None of this was hard to see. I was able to feel with great intensity those around me. Naturally I was also very sensitive to those who were no longer "living".

I understood that the noises were the mental vibrations of this beings anger as he thrashed about the garage. The dragging of the chains is a classical noise associated with ghosts and it has been reported by every culture in the world since the beginning of time. The sound of dragging chains represented the mental shackles that "imprisoned" him or her to this lower realm. What we were hearing was highly symbolic of the tortured state of the entitiy that now inhabited our garage. The images in this beings mind were simply converted into audible sounds by the manipulation of the energetic fields. The chilling of the air near him indicated he was utilizing these energies.

"The noises are over for tonight," I softly told Mark.

"You can go to sleep he won't bother us anymore"

I could feel the warmth coming back to my body replacing the cold that permeated my entire being to the core. Needless to say and despite my understanding of our guest and his troubled position I simply refused to go into the garage unless I was escorted. Mark too refused to enter the garage unless accompanied by me.

The idea that a ghost cannot physically harm you is false!

Over the ensuing months we were to find that the thing in the garage was not the only other un-worldly inhabitant of the house. There were many more.

Despite these dimensional trespasses the following months passed quickly. Mark began his new job with the ice cream company and his work ethic made a good impression upon his boss. My pregnancy advanced well and I could feel the baby kicking herself awake on a daily basis. I continued with my job at the doctor's office and reveled in my newfound life.

Request for Readings began to multiply. People found me via word of mouth I suppose. I found myself very busy scheduling readings where I could. It became apparent that Deanna was doing quite a bit of talking about me. I didn't mind. I was happy to help people. I felt I was given a special gift from God and I also believed that the gift should be shared with others.

I set an appointment to meet with one of Deana's friends the following Monday. I would meet with Jasmine at my home. I didn't charge for readings and at that time felt that anyone who charged others for a God given gift had to be a charlatan.

I must admit that through the years I have re-thought this idea. Certainly for a part time "reader" not charging for the reading is appropriate when the reader has another form of income. It is only when an Intuitive begins readings full time that it may then become appropriate to charge. If an intuitive forsakes their primary conventional job, but still requires an income to survive, then the job of being a full time Reader must produce an income. It's a matter of choices.

But I also ask myself if under any circumstances is charging for a reading appropriate. Is this what God had in mind when he allowed me these special abilities? In today's society normally both spouses must work. Would it be wiser for me to help only a few people when I could help many? With every decision there are ramifications, both good and bad. The question became quite a dilemma for me, one that I find myself questioning all the time.

Monday came and there was a knock at the door.

"Hello, my name is Jasmine" she said.

Opening the door fully I introduced myself and ushered Jasmine into my living room.

Jasmine was twenty-eight years old and there was nothing physically extraordinary about her. The feeling of despair and feelings of worthlessness permeated the room as she seated herself before me.

I explained to Jasmine that I wasn't a professional fortuneteller and I asked her how she knew Deana. Jasmine explained her relationship with Deana, but then abruptly changed gears and began crying and sobbing uncontrollably as she described the latest break up with her boyfriend.

Like an explosion in my psyche her entire life manifested itself in front of my mind's eye. In reality she could have stopped where she was because her entire past, present and future became crystal clear to me.

Jasmine abruptly stopped and looking into my eyes she asked, "Aren't you going to read cards or look into a crystal ball or something"?

I explained to her that I didn't use any intermediaries. All I needed were her eyes.

Not that I had anything against anyone who used "tools" in divination. I believe in fact that if people were to trust their abilities a little more they wouldn't need Tarot Cards or similar devices.

Appearing somewhat disappointed with my response Jasmine continued.

My chair was becoming more uncomfortable by the minute. I was now eight months pregnant and quite large. I wanted my meeting with Jasmine to be a little less formal than it was turning out to be. I felt we should have come to know each other a little better before we entered the reading. The whole of the encounter felt quite clinical.

As I struggled to change position in the chair I simultaneously threw up both hands and stopped Jasmine mid-sentence.

"Okay here's what's going on with you?"

I wanted to take my time with Jasmine and really go in depth with her concerning all facets of her life, but I was really beginning to feel uncomfortable sitting upright.

"You were neglected as a child by your Father. He wanted a boy and what he got was a girl. Because of this you have never felt worthy of adoration from any man. You have never been in a relationship longer than six months with any of your relationships. You always find a reason to break it off whether that reason is real or imagined. This is a pattern that will continue throughout your life unless you realize its systemic causes. Once you understand its origin you will be able to finally accept the love of a man"

I finally got Jasmine's attention as she bit her lip and starred into my eyes.

"Next you have imbalances within your body that causes you much anxiety, distress, depression and emotional upset. You are currently on prescription drugs that aren't needed. I will give you some advice on how to change your diet that in turn will cause an emotional change within, a change for the better. I believe that after only a few weeks of diet change you will be able to wean yourself off of those drugs."

Jasmine listened intently. Barely blinking she sat frozen to the chair. I felt I was making headway with her. But in retrospect she was an "easy read."

"Thirdly you will keep your job, but only if you change your attitude toward your boss. You are resentful of him. Within him as with all men you see the embodiment of your Father. It matters not what kind of relationship you have with a man whether it be romantic, only a friendship, or in this case your boss, your Father always gets in the way. So the answer to the question you have not asked yet is yes keep your job, but you must change your attitude because this man does not deserve the mild abuse that you direct toward him. He is a kind and caring man. If you could only return his kindness he could become a loving friend and not just your employer".

With that Jasmine wrapped both hands around her torso and began rocking back and forth in the chair.

"He doesn't deserve it" she began crying. "He's a wonderful man and I know that."

"Then you must show him the same consideration he shows you," I said. I added softly "You will keep your job of this I am sure."

I felt Jasmine understood that her job security rested with her attitude and demeanor towards her boss. Her competency wasn't in question, but her attitude was. I also felt that with a little more work it would be possible for Jasmine to finally accept the love of a man. Naturally she must first love herself, because without self-love all other love is impossible.

"And now I have to pee really bad," I said.

I struggled upwards from my chair.

Jasmine began riffling through her purse.

"How much do I owe you?" she said.

"Oh I don't take money for doing this". I replied.

With the tears still streaming down her face Jasmine hugged me and we said our goodbyes at the door. I apologized for such a short reading and told her that we would schedule another appointment at a later date. I instructed her to think long and hard about her boss and she promised that she would.

I was becoming more and more uncomfortable as my stomach grew larger as I approached my delivery date. Moving around was becoming more and more difficult and I felt that I couldn't continue with my nursing for much longer. I discussed my condition with the Doctor and we agreed that my last day of work would be eight and one half months into my pregnancy.

Janet was becoming more and more attentive as she visited on a daily basis. Sensing that my condition inhibited my ability to perform daily tasks Janet began showing up late in the afternoon to prepare Dinner for Mark and myself. I had no complaints with accepting her help and rather enjoyed being waited on for a change. Besides, Mark was basically helpless when it came to caring for himself and at this point I needed all the help I could get.

I now found myself bi-locating from my physical body almost on a daily basis. Staying within the physical was becoming more complicated. Much of my day was spent "viewing" myself from the outside. Time itself was speeding up. At times I found that everything around me was in fast motion. The apparent speeding up of time would eventually slow to a normal pace, only to speed up again. These fluctuations of time caused dizziness within me. Feelings of nausea would overcome me.

If I experienced my life review in "real time" then that would mean that I lived the first twenty-seven years of my life twice. If this were true and I lived an additional twenty seven years then this would mean that once I was sent back to the earthly plane I would be twenty seven years in the future from the point that I died? How would this be possible? My child would be twenty-seven years old! My parents would have all passed away. Mark would be an old man and the world would have changed completely. But I hadn't slowed every year down to normal time. Would any of that matter or is anything possible in this realm of spirit? I placed the thought in the back of my mind and moved on.

CHAPTER SEVEN

A Return to Heaven

I awoke that morning to consciousness piercing shards of sunlight that danced about my eyes through the partially closed curtains of the bedroom. At the same time the baby was also beginning to move and kick. I suppose she too was beginning her morning.

I was extremely large and just getting out of bed was an odyssey in itself. I finally managed to swing my right leg off the bed and push myself upwards with my left arm. About half way up I brought my right arm into play and managed to push myself into an upright position. I looked about the room for Mark before realizing that he had left for work quite sometime ago. It was a bright and glorious morning and I had a feeling of great joy and anticipation that swirled about my inner being and filled me with great happiness.

The day was filled with monotonous chores and I got dinner in the oven at five. Mark was due home by six thirty and we would settle in for a quiet evening.

That day I spent most of my time out of body. In fact I spent more time out of body then in body. I knew this was an indicator

that something very different was in the works. And then it occurred to me; I recalled that today would be the day that I began
labor. At 11:00 PM that night my "water broke" and the contractions began.

"Call the Doctor" I begged Mark.

The Doctor told Mark to get me to Peninsula Hospital immediately and he would meet us there.

The contractions came with more regularity as Mark drove toward the emergency room entrance. Looking over at him I could
see that he was just as calm and unaffected as ever. You would
think he was driving to the store for a loaf of bread!

"Doesn't anything have an affect this guy?" I asked myself.

I wondered what would happen next. Would I go through this
entire labor ordeal again? Would I be forced to once again endure
the horror of dieing on the operating table, gasping for air? As I
pondered these thoughts I glanced to my right and through the
partially opened window of the car door I could see Mark walking
through the doors of the emergency entrance.

Slightly to my right and out of my peripheral vision my attention was drawn to the outline of a person. Turning my head slightly I focused on the form standing motionless in the shadows. I
could see that it was a woman and her right arm was outstretched
toward me.

She was motioning for me to come to her.

Suddenly I was no longer in the body. I was now standing on
the sidewalk and in front of this enigmatic form that stood before
me.

We gazed into each other's eyes and I realized it was my Grandmother.

"Its time to go Kathryn." she said softly.

The love that projected from her once again overwhelmed me. I was speechless. I didn't know if I were ready for what was about to happen next, but it didn't matter because the love projected from her overwhelmed me.

"Where are we going Grandma?" I asked.

"We are going back to heaven Kathryn. You have done what you were asked to do, but there is much more to show you. There is much more for you to learn"

She then reached out to me and took me by the hand. Instantly we were projected to and flying through space. Rushing head first I could see the stars passing by as though we were flying faster than the speed of light. I looked at my Grandmother and noticed that she was smiling with great delight, as her hair appeared to be blowing in the wind. It struck a funny bone within me and I began to giggle uncontrollably. She glanced over at me and smiled approvingly. The feeling of being released from that planet called Earth brought a great feeling of exuberance.

Indeed it is a very dense and confining environment, one that the human spirit is not accustomed to. Thankfully we spend but only a brief time there.

It is not our home.

The moments passed and our flight through the space continued. What was a speck of light in front of us a few minutes before now grew into a large ball of light and we were heading straight for it. A moment later the light seemed to fill the universe and quite suddenly we were enveloped by it. My Grandmothers firm grip never weakened and in an instant we found ourselves standing in an open field. Below us and for as far as you could see were the most beautiful flowers imaginable. There were many species and most I did not recognize. The colors were indescribable. Each flower vibrated with its own frequency. Together they created a chorus that exalted the miracle of the Universe. I bathed in their beauty and their wonder. I wanted that moment to last forever. As I gazed at the unending beauty I noticed a dirt pathway that began near my feet and snaked its way through the flowers and over the gently rolling hills. I turned toward my Grandmother and found that she was staring at me very intently.

"I guess you know what you need to do next Kathryn"

In a pleading tone I asked; "Does this path take me back to Earth Grandma?"

"There is but one thing you must do before you go back to your old life Kathryn. At the end of this pathway are the answers to all the questions you ever wanted to know. You may ask the Spirits any question you like and all will be revealed to you. But there is only one hitch, it cant be promised that upon return to your earthly life you will remember it all on a conscious level. On a spiritual or soul level you will remember it all"

"Now go Kathryn and always remember that I love you and always will. We will be together again and this I promise"

I didn't argue and I can't remember if I even said good-bye. I was strangely drawn to this pathway. At that moment nothing else mattered to me. I didn't care that I would have to return to the physical. I didn't care that I was leaving my Grandmothers side. All that mattered was what awaited me at the end of the path.

With no hesitation I stepped onto the pathway and began to walk. I didn't look back and only increased my speed. On a plane where time didn't exist I felt as though I had been walking for an eternity when I saw in the distance an object. Within a matter of moments I could make out some of the details of the structure at the end of the pathway. I sped up once again and within moments the structure came into focus.

Now only but a yards in front me I beheld a very ordinary look-ing building. About the size of a small house the building was grey in color and possessed no roof of any sort. In the approximate center of the building was a door. Leading up to this door were a number of steps. On either side of the door were two very large windows. The extraordinary feature of the building was its interior lighting that could be seen through the windows. The light that poured from the windows was incredibly intense. With all the colors of the rainbow the effect was like that of a Kaleidoscope. Beams of different colored light shot through the window and into the heavens.

I felt drawn to the building and to the lights like a moth to a candle. I felt I was no longer in control of my legs as they guided me toward the steps. The next thing I was aware of I was standing on the steps. I looked down and discovered that the steps were made of wood.

"They are made of ordinary wood" I remember thinking.

I thought this very curious and turned by focus to the doors. Slowly I ascended the steps and stopped at the door. The doors too were made of wood. The door handles appeared to be brass.

With great expectation I reached for the door handle. Slowly I opened one of the doors. I was met with a blast of light coming from the interior of the building. It was as though all of the light in the universe was contained in this one building. Although my eyes were not physical I had to turn my gaze away from the light. Slowly I turned my attention back toward the interior. The light didn't seem as bright as I was able to focus and make out indistinct features of the room. I stepped through the door and found myself in the interior of the building. Just in front of me were more steps, about four in total. The interior lights were beginning to dim or, my "eyes" were becoming adjusted to its brilliance. My eyes followed the steps up. Standing just beyond the top step and on another landing were two brilliant objects. These objects though indistinct and somewhat blurred, but they were in the shape of human beings. I was able to see that they were about the same height as a normal person possessing a head, shoulders and arms. Their color was that of pure white. They glowed more brightly than the surrounding room, which still danced in a multitude of different colored lights.

As I began to fully adjust my "eyes" to the two beings of light I was struck with what I can only refer to as a tidal wave of pure love. There are no words in the English language that can fully describe the love that I basked in at that moment. Everything within the Universe was reduced to but one thing-love.

I ascended the steps. The waves of love continued to embrace me as I stopped on the landing and beheld closely what I considered surely to be the messengers of God himself.

It felt like an eternity passed before one of them spoke. His thoughts were transferred directly to my mind. The voice was neither male nor female, but androgynous. Melodic and caressing in tone the beings voice was both soothing and reassuring. I refer to them both as "he" but as pure spirit in form they are in fact neither, but at the same time both because in this state both the positive and negative, the Ying and the Yang have no apparent division or definition-they are one. In a non-physical state the laws that govern our three dimensional universe do not apply. Theirs is a state that we all are striving to reach.

As he spoke I felt that he was very familiar to me. His words awakened and stirred long lost memories and I struggled for recall.

"Kathryn, you have been on a long journey. Through many lifetimes we have helped you to decide what was the best course for you to take in order for you to grow, to learn, and to love. We have followed your growth in this lifetime and are well pleased."

The two beings that I stood before now have been with me throughout eternity. In the hierarchy of the universe they were above the Angels. And like the Angels they have never been in human form.

There are many venues within Gods mind that the soul chooses to immerse itself in so that it may grow. The Earth and other planets within our Universe and its vibratory state or level are but just one of many. The soul at its highest level and with the help of other advanced beings may choose which "house" it intends to temporarily inhabit. The Earthly plane is one of the most harsh of learning experiences. The Earth plane is reserved for hardy souls. It is reserved for the bravest of volunteers. It is also a plane where you may learn the fastest. I call the Earth a Fast Track to Heaven. It is Gods Boot Camp.

Once again he spoke.

"You have witnessed your life up to this point through a new set of eyes. We hope this has helped you because shortly you will be going back to your Earthly life where you must accomplish more things"

"But I don't want to go back. I want to stay here with you. This is my home, not that place," I pleaded.

With a voice that filled me with the deepest feelings of Love, they countered my request.

"Your life on Earth is merely the blink of an eye in the eternity of your existence and it is something that you have agreed to follow through with. You must honor your word Kathryn"

His words made me feel almost ashamed.

"But what is it that I must accomplish. What must I do to fulfill my destiny?" I asked.

"You will know what to do Kathryn for you possess all the wisdom of the Universe. You have simply forgotten many things. We will refresh your memory"

Suddenly the roof of the building we were in opened up and I was able to behold all of stars in the Universe. As I watched, all that I beheld began to move toward me. Faster and faster the stars began to rush toward me, but instead of flying past me I actually absorbed them. I was like a sponge soaking in all of existence. In what seemed like an instant I became all that ever was or ever will be. I saw the Universe from its inception by God. I knew and understood everything that was ever created or will be created. I understood every law of physics and had the answer to every question that Man has ever pondered. I saw every living form from the lowest amoeba to the highest of sentiment beings and all that they did and all that they became. I witnessed the birth of all the Suns and I also saw their deaths. I witnessed the creations of Planets and all of the creatures and plant life that inhabited those Planets. I saw the lives of every Man and Women ever born on Earth or, who will be born on Earth. I observed their struggles individually from their infancy to their Death. I beheld what mattered and what didn't matter. I also saw all of my lifetimes not only on earth, but also on distant Planets and distant realms. I saw all of our Earths history and I saw how it would all end. I saw everything that has ever occurred or ever will occur. I saw my last life on Earth and what that meant in the scheme of my spiritual growth. I saw where I would move to next.

As I stood in awe the ceiling began to reassemble itself until it was whole again. The Universal download was complete.

I was satisfied in what I must do next. My ambivalence in returning to Earth had completely drained from me. Not only was I willing to go back, but I was anxious to go back. I understood that a moment on the Earth plane in terms of growth was spiritually priceless.

I understood why a soul would choose to be born as an infant into a diseased and dieing tribe in Africa, only to die just a few short months later. In the mind of that soul every moment in the physical world was worth the pain and suffering it imparted because the soul attained growth from that experience.

I realized that every moment spent on Earth was in fact a blessing.

CHAPTER EIGHT

Motherhood

I turned my gaze toward the two beings of light and as I focused
on them they spoke once again.

"You have been given again what you were given before, but we
must warn you that upon your re-emersion into the physical much
of the knowledge you have been given shall once again be temporarily lost. Now go and understand that we Love you and await
your return"

Upon hearing these words I felt myself being pushed backwards. Softly floating just above the floor I found myself moving down the steps and out the front door of the building. I was
outside the building now and moving at an increasing speed. The
building of light became smaller and smaller until it completely
faded from view.

The next thing I knew I landed on my back with a thud, an im-
plosion of the physical state invaded my psyche. I lost consciousness. Almost seventy-two hours passed before I finally opened
my eyes. The pain was intense. I was fully aware that I was back in
my physical body. I felt heavy and dense. The existence inside the

physical body in itself was painful.

As I gazed about the room my full vision returned and I was able to determine my new location. I was in a hospital recovery room. Although brightly lit with sun and overhead lighting, it struck me just how dull and indistinct the earthly realm truly is.

I wasn't upset or mad at being back in the physical because I understood finally how important our time is here. I was going to make the absolute best of what remaining time I had because it is truly short. I would live every moment and cherish every second. I would relish even those times of sorrow and despair because each moment, each emotion, good or bad is precious.

The recovery room nurse entered with a smile that lit up the room. She walked directly to my bed and placed both hands on its side. Bending over me she gleamed a smile.

"Kathy, welcome back how do we feel today"

I struggled to speak, but the words wouldn't leave my lips.

"Kathy, I bet you can't wait to see your beautiful baby daughter"

"Where is she?" I finally managed to say.

"She is in the nursery and I believe your husband is with her. I will go fetch them both"

The Nurse left the room and I felt waves of exhilaration and anticipation pulsing through my pain wracked body.

I attempted to lift myself up with my elbows but found that it was impossible. I took a deep breath and settled back down into my bed. I starred at the ceiling and let my mind wander. I remembered that only hours ago I was in paradise, but I would make my own paradise in this realm and Katrina would be part of it.

It was difficult keeping my eyes open awaiting the arrival of Mark and my Daughter. The Doctors had filled we with Morphine that day and slowly, and uncontrollably I drifted back to sleep.

The next thing that I was aware of was Mark shaking me awake.

"Kathy wake up I have something to show you"

I opened my eyes and saw that Mark was standing near my bed to my left. In his arms was our baby Katrina. Wrapped in a white blanket I was unable to see any part of her. Mark held her so that I could finally see her face. I reached up with both arms and he slowly handed her to me. I turned her around toward me and placed her on my chest. I held her tightly realizing that my most cherished dream had come true. I cried uncontrollably for those first few minutes as I held the most important thing in my life.

"She was worth it. She was worth the whole experience," I cried out.

Mark pulled a chair up to the bed and sat down in it. Leaning close to me he said:

"Kathy, you died during the procedure. They were able to bring you back. They still don't know why you died. Shock to the heart or something they said. They don't know for sure, but you are okay now"

"None of that matters. All that matters is that she is safe and that she is healthy. I would do it all again for her" I said.

They allowed me a few more minutes with my new Daughter before taking her back to the Nursery.

I was to stay another three days at the hospital before being released. I spent as much time with Katrina as the Nurses would allow. Katrina and I entertained many family members and friends during that period and my room filled with roses and flowers of every description. I was becoming more and more accustomed to being in the physical with every passing day. I must admit my hours spent alone in bed during the remainder of my stay were filled with thoughts of those "other rooms" within my Fathers Mansion and all of the glories that they encompassed.

During my stay I asked repeatedly to talk to my Doctor. I wanted to know exactly what happened on the operating table. I wanted to know how they killed me, but the Hospital refused all request and remained silent.

I was told by a Nurse who was a very close friend of mine that I went into full Cardiac Arrest and in fact flat lined. My Heart had stopped beating for a full eight minutes. She went on to say that the Epidural was accidentally placed directly into my vein, but the records will only reflect that the possible cause of Death was an adverse reaction to the medication not malpractice on the part of the Anesthesiologist.

Though I was thankful to be alive I was mad as hell at the Anesthesiologist who inadvertently killed me. I was determined to investigate the matter further. I wasn't going to let them get away it. What infuriated me the most was the fact that no one at the hospital apologized nor even discussed the matter with me.

As a Nurse I understood Hospital policy was such that they would never admit to such negligence. In the end all evidence of liability on their part would be destroyed. I would discover this much later after returning to work and conducting a little investigative work on my own.

It was wonderful to be home. I was feeling much better, but my recovery was slow. Marks Mother Janet was a blessing in disguise as she was there every day for us. During the following six weeks Janet devoted every minute of her time cleaning the house, preparing meals, and tending to Katrina.

We all settled into our respective routines. Mark was doing well as a district supervisor at the Ice Cream company and I was happy to simply be a housewife.

A few months went by and I had fully recovered. Shopping trips to the Supermarket were the highlights of the day and I would dress Katrina in her cutest clothes for the occasion.

It was during one of these Supermarket excursions where I remember standing in line at the checkout stand when a small boy about six years of age appeared out of nowhere. He startled me by walking up and grabbing a hold of my hand. I looked into his eyes and he said nothing as we both continued to stare in silence. A rush of sadness engulfed. All of the emotion that little boy had felt during his brief life both good and bad rushed through me in an instant and I understood all of his experiences. Unfortunately his experiences were mostly negative and he was filled with much sorrow.

Suddenly the boy released my hand disappeared down one of the shopping aisles.

"What a strange and bizarre occurrence" I thought!

I have always been psychic and empathic and people on a subconscious level realized this, but this was unusual. I never experienced anything like this before and the little boys actions and the way he interacted during that brief encounter was very strange.

Over the next few weeks I found that almost imperceptibly I was becoming aware of many things I was not aware of before. It was as though a light switch had been turned on in my mind and that light was beginning to burn brighter and brighter.

I felt as though there had been a change of perceptions within me or, perhaps a heightening of those abilities that I came into this world with.

Had this Death Experience enhanced those abilities?

I do not call what happened to me a Near Death Experience. It was not a near death because I was fully dead at the time.

Just as Katrina and I were returning from our trip to the Super-market the phone rang.

"Hi Mary Ellen" I said

There was a brief silence on the other end.

"Kathy, how did you know it was me?"

"Mary Ellen, I always know when its you!" was my response, cryptic though it was.

We conversed for a few minutes when a picture of Mary Ellen's sister began to enter my thoughts. My minds eye told me that she had Cancer.

I stopped Mary Ellen mid-sentence.

"Mary Ellen, your sister has Cancer"

"What" she gasped.

"I said your sister has Cancer and it's in the Liver"

Mary Ellen was obviously stunned. Her sister Mira was only

thirty-eight years old at the time.

"Oh my God Kathy we just found out. I haven't told anyone yet, how did you know?"

I also knew that her Sisters Cancer was terminal. She wasn't going to recover from this. I wouldn't tell Mary Ellen because I hoped I was wrong, but this is what I saw.

I realized that my ability to "know" certain things had become much stronger.

On top of everything else the Spirits inhabiting our house began to become more active.

One day as I sat folding clothes on my bed I was startled by a young boys voice. The voice was close and I nearly jumped off the bed upon hearing it.

"Mommy, Mommy" he cried.

Looking up I was stunned to see a young boy standing near the end of the bed. This young entity was fully solid, just as solid as you or I. He was looking directly at me. He appeared to be about six years old and was wearing what appeared to be contemporary dress. He wore a long sleeve plaid shirt and blue jeans. I don't know if he confused me with his actual Mother or, was he perhaps asking me for help in locating his Mother?

Just as I gathered enough strength to respond to him he disappeared, dissolving into thin air before my eyes.

I decided not to tell Mark of the experience I just experienced. Certainly Mark had heard noises in the house before but I was not going to upset him further by telling him that we now had a young boy looking for his Mother.

The out of body experiences increased greatly. I would be engaged in the most mundane of chores and suddenly I would find myself out of body and observing myself from the a few feet away. I thought it peculiar that I could be out of body observing my physical body as my physical body went about its chores.

It was during one of these out of body episodes when again I received a call from Mary Ellen. Jumping back in my body I quickly acclimated to the physical and picked up the phone.

"Hello Mary Ellen" I said.

"Kathy, how in the hell did you know that it was me again?" she said in disbelief.

Mary Ellen explained that she had a friend who was having marital problems and needed some questions answered.

"She's willing to pay you for your time Kathy" she said in a pleading tone.

As I have noted, I did not believe in charging people for readings. Mark was making fairly good money but we still struggled to make ends meet. I must admit I was truly torn in making any decisions to charge for my time. I also entertained the possibility that by charging for my abilities I ran the risk of losing them.

"Ok, I will do it. Your friend can choose her time, and pay me for what she thinks it was worth"

The rain beat upon the shingled roof of our house in its unrelenting downpour that night. I sat transfixed on the living room couch watching the beads of water snaking their way down the windowpane. As I watched I fell into a trance like state. I felt the customary vibrations begin to fill my body. The vibrations were a prelude to dislocating from my body.

Just then a knock came at the door. I shook off the vibrations, and quickly rose from the couch.

I opened the door and beheld a thoroughly soaked young lady desperately attempting to shake the rain from her hair.

We locked eyes and she very sorrowfully exclaimed: "Hello, I'm Marcy, we had an appointment at two!"

I ushered her in and helped her off with her coat. I quickly showed her the way to the bathroom and handed her a towel.

Marcy spent the next few minutes drying off and attempting to compose herself.

As I sat waiting for Marcy, many scenes began to unfold in my mind. I saw a very handsome man who I knew to be Marcy's husband. I saw that this man was having numerous simultaneous affairs. Not only were these affairs with women, but they were also with men. My impression was of a man who was addicted to sex. I realized that this reading was not going to be easy.

Marcy seated herself and wasted no time as she began to tell me all about her current situation.

Marcy was aware of at least two affairs that her husband had in the past. Both women were now out of her husband's life. She went on to say that he admitted to these affairs, but promised to never make the same mistake again. She said she accepted this and de-cided to remain with him.

She continued to talk and as she did images of buildings con-taining multiple private rooms began to materialize within my mind. Within these individual rooms were many men. The men were mostly nude and they were having anonymous sex with each other. I was able to see Marcy's husband in one of these rooms, he was engaged with a number of men at the same time. Marcy's husband was a frequent visitor to the San Francisco Bath Houses.

My attention drifted back to Marcy when she asked me if I thought he was having another affair.

I didn't know what to say. On the one hand I felt I should be perfectly frank and honest with her, but on the other I knew that by telling her what I was seeing I would certainly alter the course of her life. And what if for some reason the images I was seeing was wrong? I could affect not only Marcy and her husband's life, but also the lives of their children and quite possibly many other lives. I was certainly now in a bad place. I floundered for an answer. It became very evident to me that by having Marcy place her trust in me I was taking on a great responsibility. But I could also affect my own life and my future lives via the law of Karma.

I decided to take the middle ground.

" I feel that it is possible that your Husband could be having another affair. I can only tell you to follow your own intuition. I can guide you, but I believe that you know the answer to this question already. I feel that you must investigate the matter further in order to place your worries aside. Take him at his word but you must confirm his word also" I cautioned.

Marcy hesitated for a moment and then explained that she already spoke to a Private Detective, but felt that if she enlisted his help it would only confirm her distrust of her husband.

I explained to her that in order to resolve the matter one way or another it was imperative that she seek help and resolve the matter.

She agreed to hire the Private Detective and put the matter behind her.

Marcy rose from her chair and appeared satisfied with the reading. She reached for her purse and pulled out her checkbook.

"How much do I owe you?" she said.

"Put your money away, that one was one the house," I responded.

The rain had subsided and was down to a drizzle when Marcy left. As I watched her walk down the sidewalk and to her car a wave of nausea overcame me. The nausea I was feeling was familiar to me and had nothing to do with Marcy or her problems.

"Could it be?" I thought.

Mark and I planned for a second child and we used no form of birth control. I made a mental note to pick up a Pregnancy Test kit the next day.

The following day I tested positive. I broke the news that night to Mark and he was delighted. We celebrated at our favorite restaurant that evening.

The weeks passed and additional testing revealed that we were to have a second daughter. We decided we would name her Kimberly.

When the time came for me to deliver I must admit that I was on pins and needles. Kimberley was taken by C-Section and there were no problems with the delivery this time.

I was discharged from the hospital and we returned home with our new Daughter. Once again Janet was there to help. Janet poured her heart and soul into her two Grand Daughters and once again I thanked God for her help. Katrina was now old enough to understand that she had a new baby sister and she too did her best to help out.

I was exceedingly happy. Although I enjoyed working and having a career, it was the role of Motherhood that fulfilled me completely.

As time passed Katrina developed into quite the young lady. Months earlier Kim began taking her first steps and was now talking, or rather babbling, non—stop.

With two Children and a house to maintain we found that money was getting tighter and tighter. I contemplated the idea of going back to work full-time. As luck would have it and with synchronicity working its magic I heard that the local hospital was looking for a Trauma Nurse to work on a crash team. I discussed the idea with Mark. The position was on a swing shift, which meant I would have to be to work at four in the afternoon. We spoke with Janet and she readily agreed to watch the girls until Mark got home at six. To be perfectly honest I was rather anxious to get back to work. I loved staying home with the girls and being a Mother, but working the swing shift would allow me plenty of time with the girls and time for my career also.

Two weeks after applying for the position at the hospital I was notified that the job was mine. I would start the following Monday.

I was excited but at the same time a little apprehensive. Although I never worked on a resuscitating team before I knew what the job entailed.

Monday came and I prepared the house for Janet's arrival. I pre-cooked the girl's dinner and laid out their pajamas. The girls understood that I had to go to work and they were all right with it. They could visit with their grandmother for a few hours daily, and at night their Father would be there to tuck them in.

Janet was there at three and I said my goodbyes to the girls. This would be quite a change in my life. From full time Mother to working on a resuscitating team at one of the busiest Hospitals in the Bay Area meant quite a change in roles.

At four I was dressed in my Uniform and I reported to the head Nurse. I was introduced to the other Nurses and the Doctors who I would be working with. My primary job was that of EKG technician. I made myself familiar with all of the equipment and the general layout of Emergency room. Although my duties would take me all over the hospital, it was the Emergency Room where I would be working the majority of the time. I had hoped that the night would be a slow one so that I could better orient myself, but as I would discover the night would prove to be one that I would never forget.

About a half hour into my shift we received word that there was a freak motor vehicle accident on the San Mateo Bridge. In fact the accident was so bizarre and unbelievable that it made National and International news. A young Mother who was driving a mini-van with her three children in the back seat struck a three-foot long metal rod called Rebar. The Rebar was lying in the roadway and possibly fell from the rear of a construction vehicle. Rebar is used in the cement constructions and acts and is intended to strengthen concrete. Apparently the woman's vehicle contacted the Rebar causing it to pierce the bottom of the mini van, driving it through frame and impaling her. The rod entered her body near her anus area and lodged in her intestines. Miraculously she was able to stop the Van and a passerby called for an Ambulance. The Ambulance was now approximately five minutes from the Hospital and they were now advising that the woman had just coded.

Controlled pandemonium in the Emergency Room set in. An EMT was straddled over the woman, compressing her chest as the gurney was pushed into the Emergency Room. Nurses and Doctors moved in all directions as the lifeless woman was taken off the gurney and placed on the table. About a foot of the rod was visible as it protruded from the rectum area and through her blood soaked jeans.

I struggled to gain composure as I placed the electrodes on her body. My machine came to life and indicated she had flat-lined. The Doctors gave her numerous injections and an I.V. was started. One of the Doctors made ready the Defibrillator and brought both paddles to the ready.

"Clear" he yelled

The Defibrillator pulsed and the lifeless woman jumped into the air.

All eyes turned to the EKG, which was still flat.

"Clear" he yelled again, this time not so loudly

The victims incurred massive internal injuries and much blood loss.

After many attempts to revive her, the supervising Doctor solemnly called her time of Death.

I gazed into her lifeless eyes and a million thoughts entered my mind.

It occurred to me that she was exactly where she was supposed to be despite conventional thought that dictated the opposite view. I gazed above her body and thought she must be staring down at the scene below.

In a low voice I instructed her to go toward the light. I told her that her family would be fine. I told her she had nothing to fear for it was her time to go home. She would not be coming back. It was a done deal. There would be no "bargaining" on the other side, the damage to her body was too severe.

It was meant to be.

During the ensuing months I had twenty-six people die under my care. I do not count those who died outside of the Emergency Room. Those deaths included heart attacks, car accidents, homicides, and two suicides. The suicides disturbed me the most, possibly because they were self-induced, but they were avoidable and with the proper intervention, they could have been prevented. Depression is a terrible state, and can be an overwhelming force.

CHAPTER NINE

New Friends — Old Lies

The following week was uneventful at the Hospital. It was nine in the evening and I was looking forward to getting off. The minutes seemed to drag by when suddenly one of the Nurses burst through the door.

"Kathy, they need you stat in E.R. They have a really sick one"

"I'm on my way," I said swallowing the last bit of my soft drink.

Quickly arriving at E.R. I was instructed by one to get an EKG going right away.

"What's wrong with her?" I asked

"We don't know yet she was brought in by Helicopter. She's from Samoa. She's got fever, BP is way high, she's throwing up, and she's having periodic convulsions".

I hurriedly placed the diodes on the Patients chest area.

The victim was about forty years old. With long black hair and of stocky build she contorted in obvious pain as she twisted and clawed the air. The woman was sweating profusely. She was also very pale and her breathing was extremely labored.

One of the Nurses attempted to comfort her by placing a pillow beneath her head and as she leaned forward the Patient coughed violently. The Nurse reeled backwards her face covered with droplets of mucus. The Nurse found a small towel and wiped her face. The Patients coughing continued and as I looked through the bright center light it was apparent that thousands of droplets of mucus filled the air within the room. None of us were wearing facemasks.

I got a good read on my EKG and produced a printout for the Doctor, then quickly excused myself.

We have a policy in the Hospitals that describes certain circumstances where if a Hospital employee feels they have been exposed to a possible contaminant or a person who the employee feels may be contagious, then that employee is required to report the incident. I knew of the policy, but I chose not to report the incident. I would be sorry later that I did not make a report.

The following evening I spoke with one of the Nurses present in the E.R. room the previous night. I inquired as to what the final prognosis was. She told me that the women's symptoms had subsided to the point where they released her that night. Although test were performed and some of those test were still pending the Doctors could not determine what was wrong with her.

I placed the incident in the back of my mind.

I had rotating days off and it was rare when they rotated to include a Saturday and Sunday, but today was my Friday and I was looking forward to spending a weekend with Mark and the girls.

We had the keys to my Cousins cabin in Tahoe and would leave early this Saturday morning. We all loved the Tahoe area and looked forward to spending time there when ever possible.

The weekend spent in Tahoe flew by quickly and with sadness in all of our hearts we began our drive back to the Bay Area. Mark as usual did the driving. The girls seated in the back sang, giggled and generally tortured each other during most of the drive.

I couldn't stop yawning and soon found myself asleep. The next thing I realized Mark was waking me up.

"We are here," he said as he poked me in the side.

"Here where?" I said as I slowly awakened.

"We are home. You fell asleep just outside Tahoe!"

"Oh my God I'm sorry, I don't know what came over me I just couldn't keep my eyes open" I said.

That wasn't like me.

I struggled to find my wits, but I was blurry. My muscles ached from head to toe and I was having trouble lifting either arm.

The girls were still asleep in the back seat and I struggled to get my door open. I could barely lift the handle to open the door and with great effort I managed to push the door open.

As I stood up I became faint.

"Just tired" I thought.

Mark had to take the girls from the car and into their beds. I managed to walk to the bedroom where I didn't bother to disrobe. I fell into bed and did not wake until the next morning.

I awoke early that morning and actually felt pretty good. I was anxious to get on a pot of coffee and get my day going. Mark left a note on the fridge stating that he got the girls up and was going to drop them at school.

I was thankful for this because after only a few minutes of moving around I was beginning to feel fatigued.

I drank three cups of coffee only to find that it didn't help. Exhausted I fell back into bed. I wondered if perhaps the altitude of Lake Tahoe had some sort of draining affect on me.

Apparently I had fallen back to sleep because when I glanced at the clock on the dresser I was shocked to see that it was three in the afternoon. This startled me and I tried to push myself out of bed. I was unable to do so. I lay back staring at the ceiling confused and shocked at the time loss.

Later that evening Mark arrived at home and we discussed the idea of buying a home in the San Mateo area. San Mateo was a little farther South of our present location in San Bruno, but it was also closer to our jobs. Being a more desirable area it was also more expensive. The area would also provide the girls with a better school district.

We made the decision to move. We decided to contact my Father as he was a licensed Real Estate Broker and asked if he would list the house. Father agreed and the house went up on the market.

The Real Estate market at that time was slow, but despite this we had numerous people who showed interest in the house.

Over the course of many weeks my condition worsened. Numerous appointments with Medical Specialist simply revealed that modern medicine was at a loss to explain what was happening to my body.

The pain at night was beginning to keep me awake and seemed to be getting worse.

I was forced to resign my position at the Hospital as it was becoming impossible for me to function normally.

The realization hit me like a ton of bricks that I was no longer able to care for myself, nor was I able to care for Mark and the Children.

Of all the indescribable symptoms that plagued me the most I believe it was the all-encompassing fatigue that was the most difficult for me to bear. It struck at my mind and at my soul. It was damning. I endured countless months a prisoner of my own bed. I needed help to complete the most simple of tasks. A trip to the bathroom was the highlight of those long miserable days.

On rare days when I was feeling particularly energetic I would have Mark help me into the living room where I would be placed on a strategically located chair that allowed a view of the street below. There I would sit hour upon hour.

Thoughts of suicide danced through my mind like an unwelcome guest. The more I attempted to control my suicidal intentions the stronger they became.

I knew I needed help. I remembered the Suicide Hotline and I made the decision that it would be a better course of action to discuss these thoughts with a stranger than it would with a family member or friend.

With the telephone always close by I reached for the receiver and dialed information. It took great effort just to dial the number. The line seemed to ring endlessly when finally a women's voice came on the line.

"Suicide Hotline, would you hold please?" said a hurried voice.

Before I could get out a yes or no I was placed on hold.

I clenched the phone to my chest and starred up into the heavens.

"Has God Himself deserted me?" I wondered.

I placed the phone back to my ear only to hear dead silence. After about five minutes of what seemed like an endless wait I placed the receiver back on the phone cradle.

Just then the phone rang. It was my Sister Cindy. Cindy informed me that she had a free moment and that she would be coming over for a visit.

Cindy's visits were rare and I was overjoyed that she was coming by.

"Six months!" I thought. It had already been six months and my condition hadn't improved. It hadn't grown worse either I thought. In a way that was some consolation, or was I only grasping at straws?

Cindy had her own key to my house and she let herself in. Cindy smiled at me as she made her way over to the couch next to my chair.

I could tell by the look on her face that she had something quite earthshaking to reveal to me. She starred into my eyes before she spoke appearing to gather all of her strength.

"Kathy, we have all come to the conclusion that this so called illness that you have is all in your mind. It is what they call psychosomatic! "I am not the only one who feels this way Kathy. Mom and Dad also think this is all in your head!"

What could I say? My Fathers influence on the thoughts of his

Children was immense.

Cindy wasn't the only one who believed my illness was self-induced. My Father had convinced everyone close to him that my illness was psychosomatic.

This would be the last time I would speak to my Sister for many years.

Shortly after my Sisters visit I was struck with another side affect of this strange and anomalous condition.

As I attempted to sleep I was suddenly struck with a Grand Mal seizure. Mark who was asleep beside me was shocked out of his sleep by the violent contractions of my body as it shook and bounced all over the bed. Mark had never witnessed a seizure before and about a minute into what must have been an unbelievable scene for him he was on the phone and dialing 911. The seizure itself lasted almost two minutes and I lost consciousness. The paramedics transported me to the Hospital, but by the time I arrived I was back to normal.

A battery of test were ordered and all of the usual causes of this type of seizure such as epilepsy, low blood glucose, traumatic head injuries, or infections such as meningitis or encephalitis were ruled out.

Medical science was again at a loss for explanations.

Despite my apparent deteriorating condition my Father called and informed us he located the perfect house. It was situated in a wonderful neighborhood and within the bounds of the best school district in San Mateo.

When I was able, we toured the house and decided it was perfect. Naturally we worried about the costs involved in another move. I believed it was way beyond what we could afford to pay. Mark and Father both agreed we should put in an offer. Reluctantly I agreed, but with one proviso, the offer was to be for a hundred thousand dollars less than asking price. My Father said the current owners would never agree to it. We offered the owners one hundred and fifty thousand below their asking price and the sellers accepted.

Three days later a couple put in an offer for our San Bruno home and we quickly accepted. Providence once again seemed to be working in our favor, at least financially.

Moving day came and although I was still greatly fatigued I helped with what I could. The move was smooth and seamless. Within a matter of days we were settled in to our new home.

The following weeks were particularly hard for me. I wanted to decorate our new house and many things were left undone. I was simply not able to function normally. The pains in my joints seemed to worsen. Grand Mall seizures became a daily occurrence and continuous trips to medical specialist seemed futile.

My friend Juanita who I had not spoke to for quite some time called and after learning of my condition she told me about a Chinese Herbalist she knew and highly recommended. The Herbalist was located right here in San Mateo and she offered to drive me to him.

I accepted her gracious offer. What did I have to lose? Western medicine certainly wasn't working, in fact they were unable to diagnosis my condition.

Dr. Lee's office was small and cramped. Although he spoke perfect English, Dr. Lee had a thick accent. I was told that he was one of the top Herbalists in China and taught at the University in Beijing before moving to the United States. I must admit I felt a little funny sitting in that office. I felt at the time that it was so unconventional and so foreign to everything I was accustomed to.

Dr. Lee listened intently as I described my condition. He asked me if I had been around anyone within the last few months who was gravely ill. It was like a light bulb went off in my head. I explained to him that I was a Nurse. I told him of the women from the Islands who was flown in and how she coughed filling the room with droplets as we worked on her. Dr. Lee stopped me there and asked if her condition was ever diagnosed by any of the Doctors. I told him it was not. He turned his head and fixed his gaze at the wall. In a low voice he explained that there are many anomalous viruses and bacteria that are endemic to the regions of the Islands and that modern medicine knows nothing of many of these diseases. He said it was of his opinion that I had been contaminated with some sort of unknown jungle disease, possibly a Fungus.

The Doctor took a note pad from his desk and began writing out a prescription of various Herbs. I would be given instructions for their preparation and the number of times per day I was to prepare and ingest them.

I walked out of the office with eight small bags. Each bag contained a different Chinese Herb. This will be fun I thought.

"Oh my God, what *is* that smell?" Mark was home from work and apparently the smell of the boiling Herbs was overwhelming.

The smell permeated every room of the house. My first dose of the liquid was ready.

"Not bad" I said. The liquid from the Herbs had cooled and I began taking it in. Mark watched in dis-belief as I finished the last drop.

I had faith in these Herbs and I prepared them religiously three times a day. Within two weeks I felt a noticeable difference in my body. The tenderness in my joints didn't seem as bad. I seemed to have more energy.

My partial recovery was good news too for our Mastiff by the name of Butkus. Butkus was a great friend through my ordeal and I always felt guilty I wasn't able to devout as much time and attention to him as he required. Butkus seemed to be really slowing down and because of this I scheduled an appointment with our Veterinarian.

The Veterinarian called with the news two days after our visit. Butkus had stomach cancer. The cancer was advanced and the Vet didn't give him long to live. Mark and I were devastated. The cancer spread quickly and Butkus was in much pain. We made the decision to put him down.

I grew up with dogs in my life, and consider myself a great dog lover. I cried everyday for Butkus. I truly missed not having a dog in my life. I really missed Butkus.

Mark was a Dog lover too. One day arrived home from work very excited. While visiting a friend that day, he noticed that a neighbor nearby was playing with her female Boxer. The neighbors Bitch Boxer had just given birth to a liter of pups. Mark approached the woman and inquired about her dog and pups. It was great news he told me. He said that if I agreed we would put a down payment on one of the pups and they would be ready to go home in but a few weeks.

He went on to say that the women was a truly wonderful person and an obvious expert on Boxers. The pups were all pure bred and were absolutely beautiful.

Needless to say I was very excited. I grew up with Boxers. I told Mark that he had a fabulous idea and agreed we should buy one just as soon as they were ready for adoption.

Mark promised he would keep in touch with the owner! I told him I thought that would be a good idea, but I would soon come to regret this promise and so would my girls.

We were all very excited the day our new Boxer came home. The girls were both beside themselves as they too were animal lovers. We decided to name him Jake. Jake was seven weeks old and already he displayed that incredible personality that Boxers are known and loved for.

Mark made many visits to the owner's home during the past few weeks and became very good friends with Janine. Mark claimed he was checking on Jakes progression as a pup.

Janine was in her late twenties and was married to Mike who also in his late twenties. Mark said that they were a very fun loving couple and he wanted to introduce me to them as soon as I got a little better. I agreed and actually looked forward to it. A new friendship with a nice couple would be fun I thought and it gave me something to look forward too.

The months slipped away and my condition seemed to stabilize. I continued my consultations and therapies with a plethora of Specialist. My seizures also continued and I found myself being hauled off by the paramedics on a regular basis.

I also continued my Herb therapy with Dr. Lee.

And then one day we received notice in the mail that my Health Insurance Company was no longer going to pay for any more visits or treatments. I was completely cut off by them. If I continued any treatments the expense would be completely borne by me.

I gave the news to Mark that night and he confirmed that I should continue all therapy and if we had to pay for the treatments then that's what we would do.

It didn't take long for us to go through our entire savings. To make matters worse my primary physician informed me that it was of his learned opinion that I would not recover and that the best thing for me to do was to resign myself to the idea that I was simply going to die. This hit me like a ton of bricks. I was determined more than ever to insure he was wrong in his diagnosis. I immediately began to research additional alternative methods. I recalled that my old friend Cindy always recommended the Homeopathic remedies for healing. I managed to find her old number and called her that evening. Not only was she happy to hear from me, but she also promised to come by the next day and discuss my condition. Cindy asked for Carte Blanche permission to buy anything she deemed necessary for my recovery. I of course would pay for it. I agreed and off she drove to the health food store.

My day consisted of boiling Chinese Herbs, swallowing vitamins, meditating and praying.

Slowly and surely my condition improved. Was it my imagination I wondered?

It was my habit to get out of bed around nine in the morning, drag myself to the kitchen, fix tea then laboriously walk to the living room sitting down in the oversized chair and fix my gaze to the street before me. By the time this morning ritual was complete I would normally be totally exhausted. But on this morning I was not.

It was a beautiful morning and I wondered if perhaps I should attempt a stroll into the front yard with my Tea in tow.

"I will try it!" I thought.

With exhilaration I hadn't felt in months I stood from my chair, grabbed my tea and walked to the front door. I opened the door, walked down the few steps to the front yard and seated myself near the bottom step.

Tears welled up in my eyes and I wiped them from my face. I looked skyward and noticed the sun peaking through the fast moving clouds. Its brilliance and the colors it created were beyond description. I silently thanked God for allowing me this gift.

I knew I had been brought back almost literally from the grave. The depression I had felt for so long rushed out of my mind and out of my soul.

I felt truly reborn.

I wanted to let the world know that I had made it down the steps to the front yard.

"I must call everyone." I thought.

Over the following weeks my condition continued to improve. Although the fatigue was still there I found that with each passing day I was able to do more and more.

Our financial condition however continued to get worse and worse. Mark worked as much overtime as he possibly could, but the bills kept piling up.

I contemplated getting a part time job. It had been a full two years now since I became sick. I continued my appointments with Dr. Lee and boiled his elixirs religiously. I also began acupuncture three times per week. In conjunction with these alternative methods I scaled back the traditional western treatments finding them unnecessary.

I would pray and ask God for help and He always answered me.

I was getting out of the house more and more now. Mark finally introduced me to Janine and Mike. I found them very likeable and Janine and I became fast friends.

I also began taking walks in the neighborhood. Each day I would attempt to walk a little farther than the previous day. It was on one of these walks that I met John.

Although we lived in a fairly modest neighborhood I liked to walk the few blocks that took me into the Hillsborough area. With beautifully manicured mansions the area stood as the ultimate in worldly attainment.

The first time I laid eyes on John he was cutting the lawn in front of his house. My first impression of him told me he was the Gardner and not the owner. He was dressed in dirty jeans and a white T-shirt. As I approached him on the sidewalk he stopped what he was doing, turned to me and said hello. We chatted for a few minutes and I guess he really took a liking to me since as I was to learn two of his daughters were my age. John was a top executive at a very large national Insurance Company and he had the home and property that proved his success.

I guess I gave John a condensed version of my life story during this initial meeting, but I felt comfortable with him.

"Have you ever thought of becoming an Insurance Agent Kathy?" he said.

I was stunned. In fact yes I had thought about it, but I also knew that very few succeeded as an Agent. The initial testing alone weeded out many who tried, but the actual selling of the policies was certainly the hardest part. The attrition rate was very high.

"You know I have thought about it, but I feel that I am still too weak to work as hard as I know you must," I said

John only smiled. He had such a reassuring and confident smile.

"Tell you what, I have the books you would need to study and get ready for the exam. The studying alone should take you quite a while to complete and when you are ready to test you will probably be much stronger. What do you say?"

What else could I say; yes of course I would try it.

I gave John my address and that night he delivered an armload of books to my front door.

"Here you are Kathy, study these faithfully and you will pass the test- guaranteed," he said as he laid the books on our dining room table.

"I will be checking on your progress frequently" John smiled reassuringly and turned toward the door.

As I starred at the books sitting so neatly on the table I knew that God had answered my prayers. I was not going to let this opportunity go to waste. I was determined to make it work knowing full well what my chances of success would be.

I hadn't told Mark of my plans and I waited anxiously for him to come home that night so I could surprise him with the news.

Well I had quite a wait because it wasn't until about ten that night that Mark came strolling in.

"Working late again tonight?" I asked as he closed the front door meekly behind him.

"Well yes I did work a little late. I was over at Janine's helping her with her Bitches latest liter of pups. She called and asked if I could help her since Mike would be working late again tonight"

"So how long were you over there for?" I asked.

"Just a couple of hours" Mark responded, refusing to look me in the eyes. He then turned and walked into the kitchen.

Looking back on it all I understand that I was in a state of denial during those days. I had just come back literally from the brink of death and perhaps those things that would have emotionally destroyed me in the past, I now looked upon from a different perspective. Issues that normally would have been huge shrank to insignificance in the grand scheme of things.

Janine and I continued to do things together. We enjoyed each other's company and did much shopping together. I liked Janine and I also liked her husband Mike who I considered a very descent person.

And Mark too liked Janine!

The following morning I boiled my Herbs swallowed a handful of vitamins and got the girls off to school. I then settled down and opened my first Insurance Manual.

I spent the better part of that morning studying Insurance Regulations in book #1. Not the kind of excitement I was looking for, but I was certainly determined.

Over the following weeks the Insurance study material John had given me became my Bible. They became my life during the better part of the morning and a good part of the evening, especially on those nights when Mark was "working late".

A few weeks passed and one morning the phone rang. It was John checking on my progress.

"Good Morning Kathy are you ready to test. I have some people at the Agency who are dieing to have you come to work?"

"I think I am John I have studied pretty hard and I am very confident," I said

"Okay then lets get you scheduled for the State Test and we will get you working as soon as you pass the test"

I scheduled the Exam and was given a test date for the later part of the month. The test would be given at an Insurance Commission Office in downtown San Francisco.

I was very nervous the morning of the test. The exam was administered in a very imposing high rise in the City and the testing room was filled to capacity with candidates. The official over seeing the test sat glumly at the front of the room.

I finished the test with time to spare and handed my test results to the official. The Administrator graded the test immediately.

"Well you don't see this too often," the official said as she slowly removed her glasses.

"What do you mean?" I said.

"You received 100% on your test. We don't see that very often," she said

I was so relieved I felt my head begin to spin.

I remembered that only the easy part was out of the way.

With a Life, Health, and Disability license newly in hand I think I floated down from that high rise and to the car without my feet ever touching the ground. It was an exhilaration I haven't felt in years.

John introduced me to my new boss and on his recommendation I was hired and put to work immediately. The position seemed perfect. My new office was only five minutes from home and I would be able to drop the girls off at school and then pick them up at the end of the day. Mark readjusted his work hours and would be home after school to watch the girls.

The Insurance Agency was in a large building and consisted of approximately forty-five agents, five of whom were female including myself of course. I was given a small cubicle and quickly went to work.

Since I was given no Book of Work I had to create my own customers. I began to find customers by contacting my friends and their families. I would be selling mainly Whole Life Policies with some Term Insurance, but the majority of policies sold were Whole Life.

I would also "cold call" small businesses, restaurants, and corporations. Anywhere I thought there might be a need for an Insurance Policy I found a way to get a foot in the door.

It was my second day on the job that I sold my first large Policy.

I had no problem introducing myself to total strangers or high-powered Corporate Executives. Everyone was fair game.

Of most importance I had no problem with rejection. If I was shunned it simply drove me harder the next time. Inevitably someone bought. It was a simple numbers game and I didn't let personalities or rejections stand in my way.

It was a winning combination. That first month my commissions totaled just over seven thousand dollars.

As a fast moving "rising star" within my Company I became quickly noticed.

It was near the end of my first month when the current Top Producing Agent in our office began making unwanted advances toward me. The advances, at first only verbal, escalated to the point of becoming physical. I will refer to this individual as Frank. One day when I passed Frank in the office hallway he reached up underneath my dress and squeezed my buttocks. Needless to say I went ballistic and used every swear word I could think of. I told Frank to never, ever touch me again. Frank merely laughed and continued walking.

I was very distraught that evening and Mark asked what was wrong. I told him what had happened, but he too only laughed. He informed me that perhaps I should wear something a little less alluring.

"Less alluring?" I screamed back at him.

"I was wearing a business suit Mark!"

"I'm going to bed" was Marks response and he left the room and walked to the bedroom.

I slept in the spare bedroom that night. It was the best nights sleep I have had in months.

The next morning I decided to stay out of the office as much as possible, but that was hard to do since there were daily meetings. It didn't help matters that Frank was the office manager's best friend.

In spite of all of this my business continued to flourish. I was rapidly becoming the top producer in my office. The higher ups were taking additional notice. Frank too was taking notice. The more I produced the more extreme the sexual harassment became. Shouting matches between Frank and myself became a daily ritual in the office. After a while no one seemed to pay attention. Frank was well liked by his co-workers, but I believe they also feared him. Certainly he was the alpha male of the Agency.

But I was not to be stopped and no amount of harassment would bridle my determination to succeed.

Success is borne from hard work. It left little time for other pursuits. I felt as though my every waking moment was spent pursing the sale of Policies. I felt a profound guilt that I spent so little time with my Daughters. I didn't feel this way about Mark. Besides, Mark didn't complain that he rarely saw me. Mark had many Hobbies that kept him busy when he wasn't working. His favorite pastime was riding his Mountain Bike. He spent many hours and rode many miles on that Bike.

Though we were very short on money and struggling financially Mark nevertheless found a way to treat himself to a twelve hundred dollar custom Bicycle complete with the appropriate designer riding apparel. Naturally I went ballistic, but my outburst fell on deaf ears.

I received a call from Janine at the office one morning. Her sons Birthday was coming up this Saturday and we were all cordially invited.

Naturally I accepted. I was working very hard at the Office and a Birthday party seemed just the ticket. The girls were thrilled too knowing they would be spending some time with me.

It was a small party. Janine and her husband Mike together with another couple and their children made for cozy get together.

We were all gathered in the kitchen where what was about to occur I would not have believed had I not seen it myself.

As Mark attempted to pass by Janine, Janine gave Mark a body block with her shoulders promptly stopping him. Mark spun back around. Both were giggling at this point. Mark held up both hands and reached out toward Janine's breasts, the same large breast Mark had made mention of in the past.

Just then Janine yelled out; "I dare you I just dare you Mark."

We all stood transfixed.

Janine reached down with her right hand and grabbed Mark by the groin and locked on.

In response Mark placed both hands on Janine's breast and began fondling them.

I turned my gaze to Mike who watched in stunned disbelief. As we all stood waiting for the other person to do or say something I could not restrain myself any further. The mutual groping continued for the next few seconds. I didn't waste any time as I grabbed both girls by the arms and quickly ushered them to the front door. As we went down the steps toward the car both Mark and Janine ran after us, crying out for us to stop.

Janine who was now in tears explained that they were merely "fooling around" Mark pleaded that "it meant nothing" and that they were only playing.

Mike too attempted to calm me and begged me to come back into the house.

"Doesn't this upset you Mike?" I yelled at him.

"I think they were just playing around Kathy" was his response.

But Mike was a kept man. Mike worked at a large Supermarket as a checker and had no money. Janine's family was rich. Any toy that Mike desired was given to him. It was not his place to complain, he had too much to lose.

That night my temper got the better of me. Marks rebuttal was that it was only my imagination. It was impossible to elicit any sort of emotional response from Mark under any circumstance. Once again it was a one sided argument.

I was pretty much sure at that point that he and Janine had been having an affair. My only question was for how long.

This was a life changing point for me as I look back now. I was seriously considering leaving Mark. I contemplated my next moves, but in doing so I worried greatly about the girls. I didn't want them to be the products of a broken home.

The next few days were filled with much contemplation and I arrived at a few conclusions. I contemplated what my next move would be.

I arrived at many conclusions over the next few days. I had to be honest with myself. I concluded that Mark was simply a result of my first marriage to Larry. Larry was the complete opposite of Mark. Larry was extremely demonstrative, emotional and violent. Mark never angered, was void of any emotion and didn't have a violent bone in his body. My choices in husbands were simply the extreme ends of a broad spectrum.

My most profound question to myself was whether or not I ever loved Mark?

My second question was whether or not Mark loved me?

And thirdly, was I truly wounded and hurt by Marks improprieties?

I reasoned that Mark lacked the capacity to love anyone. I believe he was incapable of loving and merely mimicked the correct emotional responses in a given situation.

The day after the party I informed Mark that I would from this point forward sleep in the spare bedroom and on a permanent basis.

I would respect myself though he obviously did not.

CHAPTER TEN

Greener Pastures

My portfolio of clients at the Agency continued to swell and within nine months of beginning work I was now officially the Top Producer in the Company.

Congratulations were in order and John planned a dinner party with some bigwigs who were flying in from New York and wanted to meet me.

I was overjoyed. I had worked very hard. News that I was Top Producer spread quickly within the office and all of the female Agents wanted to personally congratulate me. Many of the male Agents did also, but many refused or couldn't be bothered. Frank who heard the news only increased his harassment of me with innuendo, jesters and mocking.

I was told by many that this was the game I had to play and that if I wished to continue working in a "mans world" I would have to play by the rules, and so I did. Frank was the bad that always comes with the good. I agreed to go along with the program by keeping my mouth shut.

I became very good friends with one of the girls in the Agency.

Maria was from Mexico and had extraordinary talents as an Insurance Agent. She was highly driven to succeed and I believe this is one of things that attracted me to her. We often had lunch together comparing notes and talking regularly by phone during the nights.

One night Maria told me that she had brokered out to a very large National Insurance Company. The Company sold primarily disability Insurance. She said she was making tons of money selling this form of Insurance and she was easily able to handle both Agencies. She encouraged me to come on board and I did.

I was now selling Whole Life, Term, and Disability Insurance through two Companies. The money rolled in. The girls would now have anything they ever desired and so could Mark.

Life on the home front wasn't bad. For the girls sake I decided I would reconcile with Mark. In doing so I re-created a façade of the happy family. But on the inside I was mortally wounded and the wound festered.

Mark was happy as long as he was able to buy his toys. Nothing else seemed to matter to him. It brought life to his soul where nothing else could. He would also admit he was seeing Janine and Mike again.

"Its merely a friendship" he said reassuringly.

It didn't matter to me what it was. There was a part of me inside that had died also. It was dead and there was no resurrecting it.

"Fine" I said. "By the way, Katrina's B-day is in two weeks, ask Janine and Mike if they would like to come".

"I'm sure they would. Janine is anxious to be friends again," Mark countered.

I was quite sure she would. Mark was unaware that I ran into someone who knew Janine very intimately. Although no longer friends with Janine she told me that seducing others husbands was Janine's favorite pass-time. It was of course no surprise to her that Janine was also going after Mark.

I rented a public pool for Katrina's birthday and we invited everyone we knew. It was a bright and beautiful Saturday and there were more kids and adults at the party than I could count. Lunch was catered and all were having an incredible time, including my Parents.

It was just before lunch when my Father approached me at the end of the pool.

"You better keep an eye on your Husband" he warned.

"What do you mean?" I asked

"You see that blonde he's sitting next to over there, the one with the big boobs?"

"That's our friend Janine." I whispered.

"Well they have been making eyes at each other and playing "grab ass" for the last half hour" he cautioned.

I decided I would move a little closer to where the two of them were. Walking slowly I inched my way toward their position. By this time Mark was laying on his stomach near the edge of the pool and Janine was straddling his back. Janine was very busy giving Mark a back massage.

I said nothing and worked my way back to the area where the lunch was being served.

I must admit that it didn't bother me. It merely emboldened

me. It was that moment when I decided I could no longer live like this. I decided then and there to leave Mark, only I would choose my time.

Sunday was uneventful and that night I enjoyed a good sleep. I was up early that Monday morning, but I felt unsettled. Something nagged at me, something I really couldn't put my finger on. It was a feeling of dread.

I was in the office at nine Monday morning right on time for the ritual they called the daily office meeting. The meeting was somewhat short that morning and I sat directly across from Frank who appeared oddly strange. Franks face was blank and imparted no clue as to what he was thinking. As soon as the meeting ended I picked up my briefcase and headed for the car. I stopped to speak briefly with Maria before entering the elevator and proceeding to the lower level parking garage and my car.

I walked quickly to my Mini Van and opened the sliding door on the side. I tossed my briefcase onto the floor and was about to slide the door closed when I was pushed violently from behind. The incident was so sudden I didn't have time to brace myself with my arms as I was hurtled onto the cargo space of the van. I felt someone pulling violently on my dress in an attempt to pull it down from my waist. I struggled to turn myself over so that I could confront my attacker head on. I managed to get turned around but I was still on my back. Standing above me was Frank who was now attempting to pull my dress up toward my waist.

"I got you now" Frank screamed.

I kicked at him violently with no seeming affect. He grabbed me by my shoulders and lifted me partially up and off the Vans floor pushing me backwards in an attempt to move me farther into the cargo area of the van. I began screaming and pulling at his hair. Having moved me a little farther back into cargo area, he now brought both his legs into the van and was in a kneeling position over me. I continued kicking and spat on him numerous time, but he was much stronger than I. After what seemed like an eternity one of my wild kicks found its mark in his groin area.

"You son of a Bitch" he howled. Like a Banshee he turned his head skyward and continued to howl. I quickly moved to his right and exited the Van. After running a few feet I began screaming at the top of my lungs.

Hurt and obviously frightened, he grabbed his groin area and ran toward the elevators.

I wasted no time in finding my purse and retrieving my keys. I started the engine to the Van and drove at top speed out of the garage and onto the street.

Driving directly for home I nearly crashed through the fence to my yard in an attempt to park the vehicle. I ran screaming up the walkway and into the house. Mark was home and came running into the living room where I now lay on the floor crying hysterically.

"What the hell happened to you" Mark said, as he knelt over me.

"That son of a bitch tried to rape me" I cried out.

"Who tried to rape you" Mark asked

"Frank, Frank tried to rape me"

It was sometime before I could speak coherently. Mark made me a small glass of Scotch and set it down beside me. I couldn't drink it.

I explained to Mark in minute detail what had just transpired. Mark was unaware of Frank and his advances. I didn't want to Mark to know anything because I felt I could handle Frank myself. I thought Mark would confront Frank had he known of the continual harassment and it was a situation I wanted to avoid.

I was wrong about Mark.

"You can't wear those kind of clothes at work" was Marks words of wisdom.

"What the hell are you talking about Mark I'm wearing a conservative business suit. This man just tried to rape me in the parking lot" I cried.

"How do you know he tried to rape you?"

I stared in disbelief. Mark was now calmly sipping my drink.

"Well aren't you going to do anything?" I yelled out at him.

"What do you want me to do? I can't do anything, it would be illegal and if I did do anything it might destroy my chances of getting on with the Police Department"

"With the Police Department, what Police Department?" I asked

"I have decided to join the San Francisco Police Department. I just received a notice for testing," he said.

"Well that's news to me and what about this man who just tried to rape your wife, what are you going to do about that?" I asked.

"I'm going to fix myself another drink and then we will discuss it, but I wouldn't do anything too hasty if I were you, you don't have all the facts, do you? You have to be sure about these things, especially something of this nature, you just can't make hasty moves," he warned.

After a few minutes I began to gain my composure. Mark sat on the couch staring at me as though there was something wrong with me and he was attempting to figure it out.

"I think we should both get a good nights sleep and things will look differently in the morning" he advised.

I poured myself a double Scotch and quickly emptied the glass.

"Braveheart" I thought. I have a Braveheart as a husband. I made myself laugh with that thought. The liquor obviously was having the desired affect.

I was becoming calm now and decided to call Jennifer. I told her of the incident and she advised me to call the Police.

"This man tried to rape you for Christ sakes!" she cautioned.

I thanked her for listening and explained that I was very tired and needed to go to bed. In reality I wanted to call Maria and get her advice.

I called Maria and she listened intently. I valued Maria's advice and decided early on I would follow whatever direction she gave me.

"The man is a monster Kathy, but you must not call the Police yet. Let me make some phone calls and we will talk tomorrow. Get some sleep and I will see you at the office in the morning if you are up to it"

We said our goodnights and I went to bed. I actually slept really well that night and awoke the next morning refreshed and determined.

I did not go in to work that morning. Maria called early and her advice to me after speaking to numerous acquaintances in the business was that I should at least make a report to the Corporate Office. She went on to say that a call to the Police was a judgment call on my part.

I had much to think about.

I spent the rest of that day in contemplation. I made the decision to compose a report and forward it to Corporate. I would decide later if calling the Police were the correct thing to do.

The following day I proceeded to the Office and walked directly to the Manager. I explained the entire incident to him and demanded that a report to Corporate be made.

It was as though I had lit a fuse on a bomb. He pleaded with me to keep silent promising that he would handle the situation and that he personally would see to it that it would never happen again. I stood my ground and informed him that if he didn't make a report or I would go to the Police and let them handle it.

With this he rose from his chair and actually fell to the carpet. On his hands and knees with both hands clasped as if in prayer he begged me not to make a report.

"You don't understand the can of worms you are opening up here Kathy. I promise you have no idea, please, please, let me handle the matter without a report" he begged.

I was utterly shocked. As I left the office I turned and warned him;

"File the report or I am going to the Police. I will be taking a week or two off. I expect to here from you shortly"

He was still on his hands and knees when I turned and left. With head hung high I walked through the office to the elevators. Frank was conspicuously absent and I can only assume that he was in hiding.

I had much on my plate that week because no sooner did I leave the Agency and my Cell phone rang. I opened the cover and placed it to my ear, but before I could say hello I heard a woman's voice.

"Mark?" then once again, "Mark, hello?"

"Hello, Who is this?" I responded

"Uh, this is Janine" was the reply.

"What are you doing calling Mark on my phone Janine?" I said.

"Oh hi Kathy. Mark called my Mother and I was calling him back," she said.

I hung up. I had Janine's Mothers number in my cell phone book.

I immediately called Janine's Mother. She answered and I asked her if she was able to get back to Mark. She informed me that she didn't know what I was talking about. I excused myself stating that there must have been some sort of error or communication problem.

I was fighting a two front war. I needed a final resolution to one of them and the errant phone call from Janine was the final straw.

But first I needed a little more "evidence". I called my long time girl friend Jennifer and together we devised a plan. I would invite

Janine to dinner at a local restaurant. I wanted Jennifer there too. Jennifer readily agreed.

Friday the three of us met at a little Italian restaurant in Burlingame. We found a private table and ordered drinks. We chit chatted for a while then during a break in the conversation, I slapped both hands down on the table directly in front of Janine. She was stunned. Looking her straight in the eye and placing my face only inches from hers I asked the question;

"Did you go to bed with my Husband Janine?"

Shocked and surprised, her face telegraphed her guilt. Without word she clutched her purse and quickly disappeared into the nearby bathroom.

"Does that answer your question?" Jennifer asked me

"It does indeed," I said.

Minutes later and as Jennifer and I calmly sat sipping our drinks, Janine stormed out of the bathroom and without so much as a glance toward our table she exited the restaurant.

That night Janine called me at home. She explained that her relationship with Mark was strictly platonic. I listened without so much as a word until her protracted pleading came to an end.

"Well he's all yours now" were my final and only words. I promptly hung up.

Synchronicity being what it is, no sooner did I hang up with Janine and the phone was ringing once again. Only this time it was Janine's husband Mike calling from his cell phone.

Mike was concerned that Mark and Janine were seeing too much of each other. He fretted that their relationship was something other than platonic. He had no idea what had transpired earlier this evening at the restaurant. I informed Mike that I no longer cared what their relationship was, but I was concerned for him. We had a long talk and I think Mike made the ultimate decision that he only had but a couple of alternatives. He decided he would make the best of his marriage for as long as he could.

It was about ten o'clock that night when I into the bedroom to find Mark sitting on the bed thumbing through the latest edition of his bicycling magazine.

"Guess who I just got off the phone with Mark?"

"Who is that?" he said, turning his head in my direction.

"It was Mike and he thinks that you and Janine are having an affair. What do you think of that Mark?"

"That is the most ridiculous thing I have ever heard," he said.

"I will tell you what is truly ridiculous Mark, what is truly ridiculous is that I haven't thrown you out of my house yet, now pack you bags and get out!" I was beside myself.

I quickly stepped to the closet, retrieved his suitcase and threw it at him.

"Where am I suppose to go?" he cried.

"Go to your mommies. Go anywhere, just get out, I am divorcing you"

Mark packed and left within minutes driving directly to his mothers.

Janet called me early that morning wanting to know what had occurred between Mark and I. Although she told me she was happy to have him back she had hoped we would soon be able to

mend things and get back together again. I explained to her that
he had been cheating on me and that I did not want him back. Her
explained that "men are just that way", and I would have to overlook such things because they all did it!

I wasn't going to overlook it. I had respect for myself. I didn't
want Mark back.

I immersed myself in work and in my girls. Life went on and I
felt a sense of relief. More so, I felt a sense of self worth. I wanted
to live life and more than anything else I wanted to experience
love, real love, the kind of love a man and woman are supposed to
feel for each other, not this imitation of life that had become my
reality.

I guess I was lucky in one respect; our separation was unusual
in that it was extremely amiable. There was no fighting. We decided we would be very civil with each for the sake of the girls. We sat
both girls down and informed them of exactly what we were doing. They both fully understood and appeared okay with it. Mark
would visit them as much as he could and of course that included
full weekends.

I hired an Attorney for the Divorce. Mark and I agreed there
would be no court battles. Papers would be drawn up describing
who got what and what the terms of the divorce would be. If we
both agreed to the terms the document would be executed and the
Divorce would be finalized in six months. Some corrections to the
terms were made, we both agreed on the final draft, and we both
signed the documents.

We both felt it was important that the girls remained in the house until they graduated from High School. I would maintain possession of the house until that time, at which time the house would be sold and the proceeds split appropriately. Mark also decided it would be appropriate for him to pay child support. I was shocked at his civility through this entire proceeding, but somehow I think to a degree he too was relieved that it was all over.

I congratulated myself. I had one problem settled, but an even bigger problem loomed, one that meant the financial survival of my girls and myself.

I made the most of the following days. Much time was spent in reflection and in contemplation of my immediate problem.

I decided that I simply wanted Frank removed from my Office building and placed in another. I didn't care to see Frank prosecuted nor even fired from his job. I simply wanted him out of sight.

The following Monday I received a call from my Office Manager. He had filed the report with Corporate and a determination was made. I was to be placed in the Palo Alto Office. Frank would remain in the San Mateo office. I could return to work as soon as I felt I was able to, but I would be working out of Palo Alto.

I couldn't believe I was hearing what I was being told.

"The man attempted to rape me in your building and you are moving me?" was my response.

"Kathy, Frank was questioned also, he says you have been making advances toward him. He says nothing that you claim ever happened, and by the way you have no witnesses to your alleged incident"

"Is that your final determination?" I asked.

"That's straight from Corporate Kathy"

I slammed the phone down on the receiver. I was beside myself.

I wasn't going to let this happen. I called around to friends looking for legal help. One recommended a Lawyer who dealt specifically with Sexual Harassment. I called his office that day and set an initial consultation for the following day.

I met with William in his office at three o'clock. I spent about an hour with him as he explained the intricacies and ramifications of my case. William had defended many women and even a couple of men in his career. He struck me as very capable Counselor. He would be willing to take my case Pro Bono. He also suggested a cash settlement from the Company and full re-instatement at the Agency. He would demand that I return to my office of choice.

But I wasn't interested in money and I told William of this. His advised that the only way these Companies ever changed their policies was through cash awards. Adding that it was the only thing they understood.

It made sense to me!

William advised against my going back to work.

"Tell them you are taking a leave of absence, tell them anything, but do not go back to work just yet" he advised.

I agreed with his advice and we set another time for a more in depth interview.

William was anxious to get the ball rolling quickly.

I called the Agency as soon as I returned home. I spoke to the Manager and told him I would be taking a short leave of absence. He asked that I put it in writing and fax it to him. I promised him

I would.

I took a deep breath and contemplated my immediate future. I had enough money coming in on my residuals alone and if I was frugal I would be able to manage financially.

After all, I was still selling Disability Policies for the other Insurance Company. I decided I would double my efforts in this area of Insurance. The commissions for each policy were very profitable and the renewal amounts were extremely good. All was not lost. I could make a lot of money with the Disability alone I reasoned.

I received a call the following day from Mark. He was very excited.

"Kathy, let the girls know that their Father is going to be a Police Officer. I start the San Francisco Academy the first of the month!"

"Well that's just wonderful Mark" I said.

"It's a good thing I'm divorcing you cause I would never, ever be married to a Cop"

Its not that I hated Cops, I just didn't want to be married to one. I heard all the stories. The carousing, the drinking and the high Divorce rates did not appeal to me.

But Cops and Fireman were good candidates for those requiring Disability Insurance. And this particular Policy was just what the Doctor ordered. It was inexpensive, paid well when its holder had become disabled, and was issued by a Triple A rated Company.

The idea of selling to Police and Fire had not occurred to me until I received a call from a San Francisco Fireman. The Fireman had purchased a Life Policy from me months before and was now interested in a Disability Policy. I informed him that just so happened I had an excellent Policy I could show him. He asked if I could come down to the China Town station right away. I told him I could and I met him there the next day.

The Fire Station was rather interesting. Old and cramped it was nestled in the center of the China Town District. It was truly a functioning relic from the 1800's

We seated ourselves at a very large table in the kitchen area. As one of the Firemen prepared the nightly meal I quickly explained the policy. As we spoke other Firemen positioned themselves nearby and listened intently. Before I knew it we had every Fireman in the Station gathered round us. I wrote fifteen policies that afternoon and only stopped writing because I ran out of applications. I promised them I would return and the next day. By the end of the following day I had written the entire Station.

Those two brief visits netted me thousand of dollars on initial commissions and future residuals.

It was a no Brainerd. I had lots of eager customers who literally stood in line to buy what was truly an excellent Policy.

A light went off in my head. The City and its contingent of Firemen and Police were a virtual Gold Mine. I would have to find a way to get into all the Stations, both Police and Fire.

I called Maria and explained to her what just occurred. I invited her to become my Partner and together we would work the City. Maria accepted and we met the following day for Breakfast.

There was another Police Officer who worked out of one of San

Francisco's district stations. He too was interested in a Policy. He worked the Day Shift and we decided to pay him an unannounced visit.

We arrived at the front desk of the Station and informed the Policewoman behind the window that we were looking for a specific Officer. Luck was with us because the Officer was at the Station on a break. She called him and he quickly ushered us inside. We sat in the break room and I explained the Policy to him. Other Officers seemed interested too and sat nearby listening intently. Police Officers are inherently nosy people. Most do no want to be left out of what they consider a "good deal". So on that day Maria and I wrote another ten policies. We split the proceeds between us.

We were told that we had an extremely good product. Word spread quickly. One of the Officers asked if we could come back explaining that we could "make a killing" selling to the other shifts. But there was a big problem. We would first have to get permission from the higher ups, preferably the Captain of the Station.

"How do we do it?" I asked.

"Stay here. Let me talk to the Captains secretary and see if we can't get you in to see the Captain" He said.

It was unbelievable luck. Everything seemed to be going right.

Moments later, the Officer returned and gestured to us to follow him.

"The Captain will see you now" he said.

We walked down the hallway toward the Captains Office. We passed a door that led into the holding cells for prisoners. As we passed we could hear the prisoners screaming at each other. It was all very exciting. I looked at Maria and she looked as though she was ready to faint.

"Smile Maria" I said, nudging her in the side.

We were ushered into the Captains Office by his Secretary. The Captain was on the phone and seeing us he held up his finger indicating he would be just a minute.

"You can sit here if you like" the Secretary said.

The Captain finished his call and rose from his chair and introducing himself to us.

We explained why we were there and what we were selling. He asked us to move our chairs closer to his desk and explain in detail the Policy.

Five minutes later we were writing the Captain a Policy. He thought it was an outstanding Policy. He also gave us permission to enter his Station any time we choose. The Captain recommended that we address each shift that came on duty. Certainly his wish was our command.

Maria and I waited until we got into the parking before screaming at the top of our lungs. We couldn't believe it. The Gods were with us.

As Maria drove I began writing notes.

"Now lets see. There are two thousand sworn Police Officers in the City not including un-sworn personnel. There are Ten District Stations not to mention their Main Headquarters at the Hall of Justice. And then we had the other Divisions within the Department. There were the Horses, Bikes, K-9, Narcotics, Inspectors Bureau, Administration, SWAT, Tactical, and the Helicopter Unit.

Have I left anything out Maria?"

"Oh my God!" Maria exclaimed.

Lets not forget the Fire Department with its additional fifteen hundred employees.

I realized of course that my prayers had been answered. I was truly blessed, but it would be much work. We would be quite busy for as long as we wanted.

Joe was our District boss in San Francisco and wanted to meet with us to go over a few things.

Over lunch Joe explained to us that twenty years ago the Company managed to get on the San Francisco City and County automatic payroll enrollment system. It was a great achievement by the Company actually. It meant that you could sell a policy to a City employee and submit a City payroll slip with it. The amount of the Policy was automatically withheld monthly and forwarded to the Company. The Policy owner therefore was relieved of the burden of writing a monthly check to cover the Premium. This was a big plus for all parties.

Joe explained that the problem up to this point was that no one has been able to penetrate the system and sell the product en-masse.

"How did you do it?" he asked while smiling ear to ear.

"Just luck." I said.

It was just Luck!

CHAPTER ELEVEN

Gang Busters

The next day Maria and I arrived at one of the many District Stations. We spoke with the Officer at the front window and explained why we were there. He allowed us in and we set up a make shift office in the lunchroom. We were armed with plenty of Brochures and began passing them out as Officer strolled in and out. We were in the middle of explaining the Policies to two Officers when the Captain of the Station walked in. He turned his gaze toward us and I could tell by the look on his face that he was somewhat shocked at seeing us there. We had our briefcases wide open, and brochures scattered all over the table.

With coffee in hand, the Captain walked over to us.

"Who are you?" he asked.

I explained who we were and informed him that we were making our rounds from Station to Station.

"Who gave you permission to come into the Station?" he bellowed.

"The Officer at the front let us in" I replied, finding it very difficult to look into his probing eyes.

"You are going to have to leave," he said sternly.

The two Officers who were seated with us stood up quickly and made a hasty retreat from the room.

We gathered our brochures and secured our briefcases. The Captain walked us down the hallway toward the exit.

"Please don't ever come back to my Station again thank you!"

It was my fault of course. I should have gotten permission and I know that now. I would have to find a way to get into all of the Stations.

"Call the Chief, he can give you permission" Maria said

She was laughing as she said this, but I thought it was a great idea. I got right on the phone.

I spoke with the Chief of Police Secretary explaining who I was, and what I was selling. I asked for an appointment with the Chief.

She put me on hold and less than a minute later she came back on the line.

"Can you be here to meet with the Chief tomorrow at three?" she asked.

"Absolutely" I said.

I couldn't believe it was that easy. I met with the Chief the following day and he thought I had a great product. He gave me absolute access to all Stations, and all Bureaus and Details any time I decided to make an appearance. I was in effect given total Carte Blanche. Just to insure that everyone got the message he put out a teletype to all units so there would be no mistaking his orders.

The Chief also suggested that I contact the San Francisco Police Officers Association. The POA was a Union that the majority of

Officers belonged to.

It was a wonderful idea. Why didn't I think of that? I called my boss Joe and told him of these new revelations. Joe suggested that I meet with the Union and perhaps as a gesture of goodwill a small portion would be given to the POA's Widow's and Orphans Fund for every Policy sold. Joe said we would try to clear the idea with Corporate and he would let me know.

Corporate liked the idea and so did the POA. The POA decided they would introduce me and my Company in their newsletter that reached every member and civilian employee of the PD.

We were in, and we were in like no one has ever been allowed into the inner sanctum of the PD. It was going to be quite a profitable adventure for all of us.

The next day Maria and I drove to the Mission District of San Francisco. I wanted to introduce myself at Mission Station. I understood that the Station had a very large contingent of Officers. Mission Station as I was to learn later was a very busy Station. The Mission District of San Francisco, formerly an Irish enclave during the 1800's was now predominantly made up of Latinos.

We entered the Station and presented ourselves at the Front Desk.

"You must be the two Insurance ladies. We have been waiting for you!"

The Officer pointed toward the side door that that led into the rear office area, and simultaneously hit the buzzer that released its lock.

Having learned from our past mistakes we asked where the

Captains Office was. We were told that the Captain was gone for the day but he would introduce to the Lieutenant in charge. The Lieutenant told informed us that he heard we were coming and suggested that we use a small folding table he had on hand and he would have it placed in a strategic area in the hallway. He explained that way we would have maximum exposure to the Officers coming and going.

We thanked the Lieutenant and proceeded to set up shop. It was a perfect location as we had total exposure to the entire building.

Business was brisk. Almost everyone wanted a policy. The Policy certainly appealed to City Employees. If an Employee is injured on the job and unable to work they are paid their fully salary by the City. Our Policy paid an additional amount as long as the Officer remained disabled. In a high-risk job such as theirs it was the perfect additional protection they needed.

That night Maria and I didn't stop writing Policies for almost a full four hours. Needless to say we were both exhausted and decided to call it a night.

As we cleared our table we heard a loud scuffle coming from outside one of the side doors. The door burst open and we observed a number of plain clothes Police Officers who were attempting to control one very agitated resister. The resister looked like a Biker type and he was obviously very determined not to be taken into custody. One of Officers had the Biker around the neck and two others attempted to gain control of his legs. The struggle continued down the hallway as they wrestled him into the Jail holding area.

A uniformed Officer was just passing and I asked her what was going on.

"Oh, that's the undercover guy's from Narcotics. Looks like they have a good resister"

"Undercover?" I thought. They looked as bad as the guy they brought in. You needed a scorecard to tell who was who.

Maria and I recovered our composure and finished packing up. The Station was like a zoo. There was a constant parade of arrested persons being paraded past us during those hours. From Hookers to common drunks, the show never ceased. One of the arrestees looked like Charlie Manson. This character they led by us howling and frothing at the mouth. Maria wanted to pack up and leave at the point but I talked her out of it.

They must have gotten the Biker guy quieted down because a few moments later I noticed that one of the Narcotics Cops, the biggest of the group and the one who had his arm around the biker's neck was now peaking around the corner at us from just inside the booking office.

He peaked again and I smiled at him. He quickly moved back inside out of sight.

A few moments passed and he came walking out. He slowly approached our desk and reached out his hand to me.

"Hi I'm Dan. Hope we didn't scare you two with our little friend we brought in?"

I shook his hand and he turned to Maria shaking her hand also.

"You must be the two Insurance Ladies we have all been hearing about?" he asked.

We told him his assumption was correct and I quickly changed gears attempting to sell him a Policy.

"Hold on a minute. Maybe I can sell you one of my Whole Life policies?" he countered.

We laughed and talked a little more. Dan had just acquired his Insurance License and recently began to sell policies within the Department. I think he saw us as a threat to his territory, even though the two Policies were quite different.

It was getting late and I cut the conversation with Dan short. I asked him if he would be interested in selling our Disability Policy and he said he was. I gave him my business card and told him to call me. With my card in hand he turned and re-entered the office.

The weeks passed quickly for me and business was brisk and non-stop. I was working fourteen-hour days and there was little time for anything else. My girls fully understood and in fact encouraged me. I would take Sundays off and spend all day with them. Saturdays Mark would pick them up usually taking them to a nearby Theatre. It wasn't what I would call real quality time, but he was always there for them and for this I was appreciative.

I was at work when I received a call from my Lawyer concerning my Harassment suit. The Insurance Company I was suing had brought in four big guns from New York who wanted to depose me. The deposition was set for the following Monday.

I arrived at my Lawyers office promptly at nine. Dressed in a business suit I composed myself for what I thought would be but only a couple of hours of questions. Little did I know that the deposition would last an entire week. I was personally told by one of the Lawyers from New York that if pushed they would see to it that I ended up in an Insane Asylum wearing a Straight Jacket. Those were his words. My Lawyer informed me that I should take seriously every threat these people made. It was understood that the Company wasn't going to let me set a precedent. I was told they would investigate every facet of my life.

The following weeks were hellish. Whether real or imagined I believed that they had someone following. I was becoming paranoid, but these people were capable of this and even more.

Three months lapsed and I received another call from my Lawyer. The Company was willing to settle with me. It wasn't a large sum of money and the Company would admit to no wrongdoing. I agreed to the settlement. I wanted nothing more than to put this chapter in my life behind me. They agreed to leave me in the San Mateo Office as I requested and they would move Frank across the Bay.

Despite all of this I never went back to that Office resigning my Agency with the Company.

I learned a few months later that the Federal Government was investigating Frank. Federal Agents entered his office with search warrants and removed all of his files. My Managers pleas to let it all go made perfect sense to me now. My suit indeed opened up a can of worms that no one wanted open. Frank fled back to his native country and dropped out of sight. My Office Manager suffered a stroke shortly Franks indictment and was himself indicted by the Feds. There were many things going on in that office that none of us were aware of. Apparently the Company decided to do a little more digging on its own.

I was glad to be gone. I never looked back.

But there was something missing in my life. Nightly meditations and occasional readings took a back seat to my long hours at work.

I accomplished my initial goal of making a lot of money and thereby insuring monetary security for my Daughters and myself. But I felt this great void, and it wouldn't be filled with material things.

I made the decision to start working a normal schedule of eight hours a day, perhaps ten if need be. I would also allow myself weekends off. I put the word out that I was once again available for readings. Life would return to some normalcy and I began meditating again nightly.

Within a few short weeks I was reading for people on an almost nightly basis. Naturally I didn't charge for readings, I didn't have to, I was making more than enough money. I did it because I loved to and because I loved helping others.

There is but one circumstance where I believe the taking of money for readings is warranted. If the reader is unemployed and is in need of money then that might necessitate the need to charge. Yes, we all need money to survive but I refused to sacrifice my gifts of discernment for a little additional income.

But I too was in need of direction at times. I could not easily discern for myself as I did for others. I found it difficult to locate a truly gifted Psychic who could read me. I had been to many self described Psychics, each and every one "read" using a prop.

I found it often amusing because invariably before they were finished with their attempt to read me I would be reading them. I think most of them were astounded by this little quirk of mine and would sit in silence as I delved into their lives and futures. Most soon forgot about the reading they were doing for me. For those who were actually gifted I would explain that the "tools" they used were unnecessary and they needed to trust in their abilities, as God would guide their thoughts.

A true Psychic or intuitive should have the ability to sit down and without asking any probing questions, he or she should be able to answer all of your questions.

I have yet to find a Psychic who operates without Tools. I know good ones are out there, but I just haven't met any. I must admit however there have been some who through utilization of certain tools have impressed me.

The public is so accustomed to a Psychic who uses Tools, that without these Tools the Psychic appears inadequate or lacking in some manner.

In reality it is quite the opposite.

Some months had passed and Maria and I had made the rounds to every Police and Fire Station in the City. The money was pouring in for both Maria and I. Maria, always the entrepreneur announced to me one morning that she would be moving on. She would no longer sell any Insurance. Maria had enough money coming in from the residuals alone to last her quite a long time. Maria announced she would be going into Elderly Care by opening up one, perhaps two homes to begin with.

I was happy for Maria, but I also didn't want to lose her as a partner.

I enjoyed having another person working with me. Besides there was enough money and business for two Agents, actually there was enough business for ten Agents!

Maria, being slightly intuitive herself had a recommendation for me.

"What about that big cop we met months ago, you know the one with the Insurance License. He would work with you!"

"You were reading my mind Maria. Actually he would be perfect. Everybody knows him. He knows his way around the Department and I think he's hungry. The poor guy has called my pager twenty times and I never returned his call. I don't know if he would want to do it now. To tell you the truth I was really attracted to him and a little afraid to call"

"I would call him," Maria said, smiling.

"Okay I will call him tomorrow, but I will bet he doesn't return my page" I said. I was a little embarrassed about the whole thing.

I paged Dan the following day and he called me back immediately. We set a day to meet and finalize our work agreement.

That Wednesday I met Dan in a little coffee shop on Van Ness Avenue. Dan explained to me that he was now working out of the Federal Building with the D.E.A. Although the San Francisco Police still paid his salary, he became a full member of the DEA's group II. I wasn't sure exactly what this meant, but he was certainly excited about it. I got the impression that he didn't care much anymore for the P.D. My only concern was if he would have enough time to devote to Insurance Sales with me. Dan assured me he would have ample time to devout to the selling of Policies and we set a start date.

I was struck with an overwhelming feeling at that moment. It was a feeling of Déjà Vu. As I watched Dan leave the shop that afternoon and get into his unmarked car it was the strongest feeling of recall I had ever experienced.

"This will be interesting," I thought as I watched Dan drive away.

And interesting it would certainly be. More interesting than I could ever imagine!

CHAPTER TWELVE

The Bonds Grow Stronger

I met Dan at the Police Headquarters on Bryant Street. It was our first day of work together. I decided to drive because I knew exactly where I wanted to go.

"Good Morning" he said as he slipped into the passenger side of my car.

Yes it was a good morning. He looked very dapper in his slacks and fitted dress shirt. With his large frame he struggled to seat himself in the car.

"Good Morning" I said, smiling brightly at him.

As I drove to our first stop we did a lot of talking, and by the end of that day I knew most of his life story.

He came from a broken home. His Mother and Father divorced when he was just eight. With his Mother and Brother the three moved into his Grandmothers home. Dan also had a sister and she moved in with his Aunt. His Grandmothers home was in an all black neighborhood of San Francisco, and Dan found that he was the only white kid on the block.

His family in San Francisco went back six generations. Dan

told me that he had always wanted to be a San Francisco Cop but now found that he was growing bored with it. I judged by his intelligence level that certainly he could have been anything he wanted to be.

I learned too that although he was married for just over a year, he was in a loveless marriage. He and his wife slept in separate bedrooms. From a previous marriage he had three sons. His former wife moved to Michigan to be with another woman and took his three sons with him. Though he tried legally to stop the move, he was unsuccessful. Much of the money he made was going to child support payments. This of course explained his need for a second job.

Dan also had a great interest in the Paranormal and had many childhood experiences living in very haunted houses.

I found this quite unusual because I knew that Cops in general were not out of the box type of thinkers and if something could not be proven factually, then it did not exist. Naturally, these interests were kept to himself.

In the 60's Dan and his friends frequented the Haight-Ashbury district. At the age of sixteen Dan taught himself how to read Tarot Cards and for fifty cents he would give sidewalk readings to anyone interested.

"How in hell did you become a cop?" I asked.

"I didn't get caught" he replied.

He continued.

"My Father was from North Dakota, part Sioux Indian. He was as tough as nails. He was a Professional Prize fighter for many years. He once fought Joe Louis. They all said he would have gone far, but he had a little problem and that problem was called women"

It was getting late and we had finished our last appointment together. I wanted to sit the rest of the night with Dan as his story was becoming quite interesting.

We said our goodbyes and I dropped Dan at his car.

I wondered if Dan might have the same problem with women that his Father did, but that didn't appear to be the case, at least so far.

"We will see," I thought.

We would meet the next morning and have at it once again. Dan was a good worker and I was very happy to have him as a partner.

We worked very hard during the following weeks. Together Dan and I spent long hours canvassing every Police and Fire Station in the City. I must admit, I was having a better time just being with Dan then I could have imagined.

I received a call from a girl friend the following day. Kay who I had known most of my life was in town from San Diego and wanted to know if I could have lunch with her. I agreed to lunch and explained I would be bringing my partner Dan. We met at a small Italian restaurant in the Noe Valley District. We finished lunch and began walking toward our cars when the strangest thing happened. I was struck with an overpowering feeling of a future event. I walked side by side with Kay and Dan was walking just in front of us.

I turned then to Kay and said; "I'm going to marry that man"

"What man?" asked Kay.

"Dan, I'm going to marry Dan," I said. I almost chocked on the words.

I spent the remainder of the day contemplating my remark to Kay. I was still legally married, at least for the time being, and Dan was still married.

On top of all of this he was a Cop!

I learned to trust my inner feelings a long time ago. As a Psychic you must trust your feelings and especially those feelings that were this pronounced.

The right side of my brain wanted to dismiss what the left half was telling me.

And so it went. The days turned into months and the money continued to flow in, but not at the rate it had. The longer Dan and I were together the more we wanted to be together. Instead of spending our time with would be clients we found ourselves discovering each other instead. The majority of our time was spent in coffee houses or at the park eating cheese and crackers and simply relishing the fact that we were with one another.

I have to admit that I was falling for him and it was pretty obvious that he felt the same.

And then it happened. Dan dropped me off at my house one night as our day came to an end. We said our good byes and as I was beginning to open the car door to exit Dan clutched my arm. He hesitated as he looked deeply into my eyes.

"I think I'm falling in love with you, I just wanted you to know that" he said softly.

I went into complete shock. I felt as though a truck had hit me. I said nothing and quickly left the car. I almost ran to my front door. That night was spent in quiet reflection of those words. I kept hearing them over and over in my mind.

I was getting ready for bed when the phone rang. It was Dan. I hesitated in answering but slowly I reached for the phone. We spoke for about a half hour and the conversation was centered on the day's work and tomorrows schedule. We said good night to each other with nothing more being said concerning what he uttered to me in the car. For that I was grateful. I needed more time to synthesize the apparent change in direction of our relationship.

I prayed that night before falling asleep. I asked my Angels for direction and help in regards to this dramatic turning point in my life.

The next day Dan and I returned to work in the City. It was just another workday and our conversations were kept light and unassuming.

When the day was over Dan dropped me at home once again. I was just finishing up Dinner when the phone rang. It was Dan. He was calling from his cell phone from his car. He was quite upset and told me he left his house after having quite a very bad fight with his wife. She accused him of having an affair with me. She revealed to him that she herself was having an affair with the next-door neighbor. This came as no surprise to Dan as he had mentioned his suspicions to me many times before. Dan too is quite intuitive, but his suspicions were solidified not only by his wife's actions, but also the behavior of the neighbor toward his wife. Dan's wife was quite tipsy with wine and the fight by throwing a glass of wine in his face.

Dan told me he didn't know where he was going to stay that night, but he also insisted he wasn't going back to his house.

"Come on over you can stay here," I said.

With no hesitation he said; "I'm on my way".

It was almost ten o'clock when the knock came at my door. I was already in bed and Kim and Katrina had been asleep for almost an hour. I directed Dan to the couch in the living room and I retrieved some blankets and a pillow. We promised we would speak in the morning and we said our goodnights. I got back in bed and only minutes had when I felt Dan's body slipping into my bed. He pulled the covers over him. I lay motionless pretending I wasn't aware of what was happening. After what seemed like an eternity Dan rolled over and took me into his arms.

"Oh God how I love you Kathryn" he whispered.

"I love you too Dan. I love you more than you will ever possibly know"

We embraced passionately for the better part of that night. I felt a love with Dan that I had never known with any other man.

The Angels had answered my prayer request. The words I spoke to Kay as we walked from the restaurant that day kept running through my mind. I was certain more than ever that indeed I would marry this man.

The next morning Dan and I discussed what our next was going to be. Dan informed me that he in no uncertain terms would never return to his wife. I let Dan know that it was all right with me if he moved in, but I would have to clear it first with both of my girls. Dan agreed and that night we gathered the girls together for a meeting.

Both girls readily agreed that it would be a good idea that Dan moved in. They even seemed excited about the prospect. It didn't surprise me since over the past few months Dan and the girls grew quite fond of each other. Dan lavished them with many gifts for their Birthdays and other occasions during those months and the bonds grew stronger.

Within weeks Dan was fully settled in and we all enjoyed each other's company. A few weeks later Dan was served with Divorce papers. I could see that with these papers an enormous weight was seemingly lifted from Dan's shoulders. Dan was being released from a marriage that was loveless from its beginning and humiliating in its finality. Dan seemed genuinely happy and there was no hiding it.

But with the sunshine a little rain must fall. With Dan's personal life improving he received news that he would no longer be working within the DEA. He was told that due to shortages within the Patrol Bureau he would be taken out of the Narcotics Division and placed back into a District Station. In layman's terms he would be back in uniform and sent to the most dangerous district in the City. This was not welcome news. But orders must be followed and within days Dan found himself working a marked "radio car" in the Hunters Point section of the City.

It was about a year after being back in uniform and on patrol when Dan received a call of a Burglary in progress. Dan chased a suspect through a backyard as the perpetrator attempted an escape. Dan took a fall and hurt his back pretty badly. He was off work for a number of days when the next incident occurred. The tire on his patrol vehicle went flat and Dan decided to change it himself. He re-injured his back in doing so and was once again off work.

This would be the last day Dan spent in uniform, and the last day of his career with the Police Department.

Test indicated that not only was his back strained but that he had five degenerative disks in his lower back.

It was recommended to Dan that he seek a Disability Retirement with the City.

Dan agreed to the recommendation and sought a full Disability Retirement. Little did we know at the time that the City wasn't very flexible in granting Disability Retirements to any of its employees. The battle for a retirement would last a full three years and during this time Dan was allowed very little money to live on.

Because of this I returned to the full time job of selling Insurance. Since Dan was unable to help me sell I found myself alone in the City working long hours once again. To my dismay the joy and excitement I once found in selling Policies was no longer there. Over the course of the ensuing weeks I began working less and less hours until I stopped selling altogether.

I threw myself into doing what I loved to do best. Every night was filled with people who sought advice and direction from readings.

CHAPTER THIRTEEN

Finding Paradise

But Dan now found himself on a somewhat extended vacation. Between visits to various Doctors, Chiropractors and Bureaucrats, Dan had to find ways of keeping himself mentally and physically busy. I too found myself with a lot of time on my hands and decided to begin selling Policies again, but not to the extent I had in the past. Now and then I ventured into the City to sell a Policy or two, but after a confrontation where I had a gun put to my head I decided to stay home. Besides, Dan was home and I did want to spend as much time with him as possible. Most of the work I was doing now was by appointment. I made quite a name for myself in the City and I received numerous calls each day to write Policies. I would meet with the client usually at their home or sometimes mine. I found my new schedule quite perfect as it kept me busy enough, but not too busy.

I also felt I had neglected my Daughters during the last couple of years and I would now make up for it.

Dan and I spent much of our time in pursuit of keeping ourselves busy. One of our daily rituals was walking Jake and Joy. Jake was a Boxer and Joy a Mastiff. Dan would attempt these walks daily, but found that his back injury would greatly curtail the amount of walking. At times he would only manage to walk a few feet before having to turn back. Sciatica was a big problem for him and has remained so over the years.

It was during one of these walks in the beginning part of 1999 that I had a premonition, a vision really. As we walked my mind filled with scenes of destruction and smoke. It was New York City. I turned to Dan and began telling him what I was seeing, as I was seeing it. Dan listened intently as I told him the following;

"There will come a great destruction. It will be centered in New York City. I am seeing plumes of smoke and great destruction. I can't see what is causing the destruction. I do know this though, it will literally change the world and it will change the world as we know it-forever!"

Dan wanted more information.

But that was all I saw. I had no idea what caused it or how it happened. I didn't know who and what was involved, but I did know that it would completely change the world somehow.

"I got it" Dan said.

"The Nostradamus prediction. In the year of 1999, in the month of July a Great King comes from the skies. He is somehow related to the third Anti-Christ"

"I don't know," I said, but I didn't think it was related to this prediction.

We both thought about it and discussed it further while we walked. It was quite a prediction. I think in the back of our minds we both thought that it would be terror related. We didn't speak of this vision again, not until it actually occurred that is.

I only told perhaps three other people of my prediction. It wasn't something you would want to tell everyone. Besides, it was so horrific I really did not want anyone to think I was an alarmist.

I had built up quite a clientele over the following months and was averaging at least two in office readings per day at our home. At night I averaged at least one more by phone. My name was spreading across oceans also. Through a friend, a movie producer in the Philippines called for a reading. This particular lady who was very well known on the Islands became a regular customer and also a good friend. It was this same year that I went out on radio Bay Area Wide. The shows theme covered included subject on the paranormal and the esoteric.

It was also during this time period that my Father re-entered my life on a grand scale. My Father had his eye on a new Condominium and wanted me to accompany him. He had grown tired once again of his current abode and decided it was time to move. He also had his eye on a small business, a Golf shop of all things. My Father felt that I owed it to him to purchase the Condo and Golf Shop for him. I reluctantly agreed to look with him the following weekend.

On Thursday of that week Katrina came down with a terrible Flu. I called my Father and advised that I would have to reschedule. Without any further word my Father hung up on me. I spent the better part of the next two weeks in a futile attempt to reach my Father. He refused to accept any of my calls. It was the last time

I would talk to either of my Parents for eight years.

In the early part of 1999 Dan proposed marriage to me. I agreed, and we set the date for October of that year. We found a beautiful Church in Woodside just South of San Mateo. The Church was over one hundred years old and was located in a beautiful country setting.

Within a couple of weeks of reserving the Church for our wedding day, we received a call one morning from an administrative employee of the Church regretting to inform us that the church would not be available in October. She did have spot open on September 11th however. We agreed and the wedding was re-scheduled for that day.

We had a picture book wedding with many friends and family attending. The wedding went off without a hitch and the next day we were winging our way to Sedona Arizona for our honeymoon.

We arrived in Phoenix, rented a car and drove to Sedona. Though we spent most of our time in Sedona, our Hotel was booked in Jerome at the Grand Hotel, which was only a few miles from Sedona. The Grand Hotel of course was reputed to be very haunted and was situated on hill of this former mining town. Jerome is filled with artsy little shops and those souls who for one reason or another are drawn to Ghost Towns. We found it very quaint and quite different from anything we had ever seen.

Sedona is one of those places that you must see before you die, it is truly inspiring. Sedona is a highly charged area, and a reputed portal to other dimensions. This area will in one fashion or another influence your thoughts and touch you at your deepest level.

It is said that dependent upon your current spiritual and emotional state, Sedona will magnify these feelings whether positive or negative. All is dependant upon your emotional state during the visit.

Our days spent there were wonderful and awe inspiring. We managed to partially climb Bell Rock where we meditated. We were also witness to some truly anomalous occurrences in the skies before and after sundowns. The little shops alone were worth the trip. I was beginning to fall in love with Arizona. I believed the State was on a higher spiritual level than any other place I have ever been.

I truly felt spiritually elevated during our stay there and did not look forward to leaving its beauty.

Dan lived in Arizona during the mid 70's and recalled once driving through Sedona when it was small town and had but one stoplight. What a difference a couple of decades makes. If you can look beyond the motorized Cable Cars that tour the main streets with the multitudes of people from every part of the globe, then you too may drink of its majesty.

Dan expressed to me his love of Arizona and told of his dream of once again living there.

We thought about the idea of moving out of California when the girls had completed High School. We presented the idea to the girls and they thought the idea was a good one.

We returned to Arizona many times that year. We were dumbfounded by the prices of the homes as compared to homes in California.

We felt that the Tucson area in particular was especially beautiful. The Sonoran Desert with its majestic Saguaro's was a sight to behold. We enlisted the help of a Realtor and begin looking at homes. After three intense days of looking, we toured a beautiful home near the base of the Catalina Mountains. The home was in an unincorporated area, but technically still considered within the bounds of Tucson. It was a Mediterranean style home, almost four thousand square feet and with a pool. Neither Dan nor I have ever lived in a house with a pool. To us the home was a dream come true. Dan didn't care for it much to begin with, but I must admit that I was drawn to it like I had never been drawn to anything before. I had to have this house. As the old saying goes; the woman decides on the house. We instructed our Realtor to put in an offer for the house.

We returned to San Mateo and received word that the sellers accepted our offer. The sellers were an older couple from Illinois. This particular house was their second home. They were "Snowbirds" and during the winter months they fled Illinois and enjoyed the winter in Tucson. We were told that the Husband loved the house and the area, but his wife absolutely despised the house. We couldn't understand her attitude at the time.

We placed the San Mateo house up for sale and we were flooded with multiple offers. With the house sold, Mark and I split the proceeds.

Our dreams were in motion, and in July of 2005 we moved to Tucson and into our dream home. We felt like modern day pioneers. A feeling of discovery and elation captured us all. Katrina and Kim were very excited to be living in a completely different environment and all of the new experiences that came with it.

Kim enrolled at the University of Arizona and Katrina began looking for work.

Our first year in Tucson couldn't have gone better. We explored the area of course and visited the artsy little towns nearby looking for items to decorate the house with.

We began a Security business also. Our Company furnished Security Guards to businesses that who required them. With Dan's expertise in the Security field and my good business sense with its never say no attitude we expanded very quickly. Before long our Business was thriving. Kim finished her first year at U of A and Katrina landed a good job in Property Management.

Life was good.

Tucson is a very ancient area. Continuously inhabited for the last ten thousand years, many ancient people have lived and died in this valley area. More than one person told us that Tucson would either accept you, or it would reject you. By this statement it is not meant that the current inhabitants will accept or deny you, but that the area itself will make that determination. The energy that permeates the area will either accept or reject.

The universe is built on sound patterns allowing numerous worlds and dimensions to exist in the same space. Each is on a different frequency. The same truth applies within individual dimensions and our interaction within the dimension.

If ones frequency is "out of tune" within a given locale nothing seems to work. It's an immutable universal law that cannot be overcome no matter how hard one tries.

We were into our second year when things began to go terribly wrong for us.

When we first moved there the people of Tucson seemed friendly enough, but that too began to change. We moved to Tucson during the height of the Real Estate boom. Money was flush during those times and everyone flourished.

At first we thought that it was our imagination, but gradually we came to understand that Californians simply were not well liked. It seemed as though the locals could spot a Californian a mile away. After a year or so we were really beginning to feel like "fish out of water"

We were also beginning to experience culture shock. What was novel in the beginning became a negative distraction that grew in intensity.

To add insult to injury, the house itself seemed to turn on us. To be more exact, those who "inhabited" our house began to make themselves more evident to us.

From our very first night in the house we became aware of strange voices. We could hear what sounded like two young girls at play with one another. The conversations we heard seemed to be coming from somewhere down the hallway. The voices were muffled and undecipherable. Over the following years many friends, relatives and even Contractors working in the house alerted us to these strange and playful conversations.

It was our second year in the house and as I was seated in the living room with my Daughter Katrina watching a Movie that a little boy who I would estimate to be seven or eight years old appeared in the hallway just a few feet from me. He appeared to have been running down the hallway and upon seeing me he came to a sliding abrupt stop. We starred into each other's eyes. I received the impression that he was shocked that I could see him. He was dressed in 19th Century period clothing and wore a white button down shirt with dark dungarees. His hair was parted in the middle and was cut in a "sugar bowl" style. He appeared as solid as you or I. I am certain I elevated from the couch because the next thing I knew I was running down the opposite hallway toward Dan who was busy at the time in the Master bedroom. Although Katrina did not witness the apparition she too nevertheless bolted from the room running in close pursuit behind me.

Both Dan and I have lived in haunted homes before so this was nothing new to either of us. Parapsychologists estimate that sixty percent of homes are "haunted". It would appear now that this home too fell within that category.

The strange occurrences began to increase in intensity. Apparently whoever or whatever was in the house with us enjoyed culinary delights. Quite often and normally around two in the morning, loud noises would ring out from the kitchen area. From the sounds made one would suspect that persons unknown were preparing a full course meal. The sounds of cabinets closing and pots and pans banging about would be heard. The sounds of adults talking and children playing and jumping were also heard. These episodes would sometimes last more than an hour and were heard not only by us, but by numerous guest spending the night in adjoining bedrooms and over the course of a couple of years.

During one occasion Janet was visiting for a few days and we gave her the bedroom near the hallway where I witnessed the running boy. Her bedroom was just adjacent the kitchen. That morning during Breakfast she politely complained that she was awakened by loud noises. She thought it curious that we would cook in the middle of the night. What confused her were the Children she thought she heard. The Children as she put it were "roughhousing" and making quite a racket.

Not wanting to worry her we suggested she was probably dreaming. We blamed it on the Desert air, as it was known to produce vivid dreams.

Janet was apparently satisfied with the explanation and promptly dropped the subject.

I must admit that none of us were ever brave enough to venture into the kitchen while this phantom family prepared their meals.

We couldn't really complain however since none of our food items ever seemed to vanish.

Dan decided he would attempt to record whoever and whatever was haunting the house. He would accomplish this by means of EVP, otherwise known as Electronic Voice Phenomena. EVP is a method used all over the world by paranormal researchers to make contact with the "other side" Its methodology is pretty simple. A common tape recorder is utilized and while its set to record, a series of questions are asked. After a few minutes of questioning the tape recorder is turned off then played back. If any answers to your questions are received it will be "heard" by the Tape Recorder. The theory is that the voices produced are above those frequencies that our physical ears can pick up, but it is not beyond the range of what the Tape Recorder hears. Obviously there are certain magnetics involved in the capture of the voices.

Dan read about the practice of EVP technology for years but was reluctant to try it. The possibility of opening a "doorway" or "window" that one didn't necessarily want open was a real possibility.

Many called EVP investigation nothing more than an "Electric Qui-Ja Board"

Dan theorized that the doorway was already open. He was determined to confront whatever was in the house and gain a better grasp of what we were facing.

Over the course of the next few months we were able to record a number of entities in our home.

There are no experts in this field. There are only those who are more adept at capturing the voices then others.

I of course consider myself among those who assume to know very little when it comes to the paranormal. Naturally God in many areas of my life has gifted me, but I couldn't tell you where these "voices" originate.

Are the voices those of the departed? Are they the voices of those who we call Ghost? Or are they living entities that reside in a nearby reality or dimension?

I do know that we can ask questions during a session and receive a direct response to the question. I also know that the voices do not originate from an errant A.M. radio station.

We are able to receive direct answers to direct questions.

Of particular interest was a recording that Dan acquired one afternoon. Dan finished his daily swim with the dogs and was changing in our bedroom when he heard what he assumed to be Kim and myself returning from the store. He said the voices were very loud and there was much giggling and laughing.

Dan quickly finished dressing and walked out to greet us, but instead found an empty house.

Dan realized that the "Girls" had once again come for a visit and were likely still present.

This time Dan had the presence of mind to quickly turn on his Digital Recorder and begin asking questions.

During the taping Dan asked a series of questions.

After taping for a number of minutes Dan downloaded the session onto the computer, then opened the session in an Audio program for playback.

Dan realized he had captured the voices of the two young girls.

On the recording you can clearly hear one of the girls whispering to the other.

"Do you think he can hear us?" There was a slight pause and she repeated the question once again to her unseen friend.

The little girls were apparently startled that Dan knew they were present. Both voices were very clear and distinct.

Near the end of the recording Dan asked once again if the two girls were present.

They answered in turn; "Yes!"

Were these two merely "interlopers" from another dimension

caught off guard and shocked that Dan knew they were there and was actually asking them questions?

Or were they time travelers and not Ghost in the general sense? Perhaps they were allowed out of their dimension to play in another. Were they given permission by a Parent to go "play" in this realm but warned to be back by Dinnertime?

Did they venture from home to home in the neighborhood in an attempt to amuse themselves?

Are the voices caught on tape manifestations from our own minds, perhaps thought projections? If true then how would that explain the fact that Dan heard the girls initially with his physical senses?

These are questions worth asking. To believe the voices are of those who have passed is to limit ones thinking.

I believe they include all of the above possibilities and many more.

Many of the entities that inhabit this other world are profane and contentious. They fight among themselves in the same fashion that we the living argue and swear at each other.

There are also good ones and bad ones.

Bill was one of the good entities. This entity identified himself to us by name during one of Dan's sessions. Bill had a slight Western accent, and by the sound of his voice he was most likely elderly.

We came to believe that Bill protected us from negative forces within the house. This belief was borne from those things said by Bill during numerous sessions.

Bill warned us of possible future Terrorist attacks. Incredibly he even gave us Real Estate advice when we put the house up for sale advising us to "take any offer that comes in".

Despite Bills presence, the house was becoming very "heavy" with the other entities that resided there. The house that I once loved became dark and foreboding.

Dan was becoming very uneasy in the house and complained he felt as though he was always being watched.

One of our biggest scares happened early one morning, as we both lay asleep. I was awakened by the ceiling light in the hallway adjacent our bedroom. A dimmer switch controlled the light and it appeared that someone or something was operating the dimmer. The light would grow to full brightness only to fade to near darkness, then repeat the same thing again. After a few moments I slowly reached over and shook Dan awake.

Dan raised his head and starred toward the hallway. Observing the light show for a few seconds was enough for Dan. Jumping out of bed he approached the fluctuating light and began yelling at the top of his lungs.

"Get out of my house. In the name of Jesus Christ leave my house now" he said.

He repeated this several times. But it wasn't over yet. I felt a chill of very cold air permeate my body and at the same time something unseen grabbed a hold of my throat.

I was being chocked, and I couldn't speak. I reached out a hand in desperation toward Dan. Dan saw what was happening and ran over to help me. As soon as Dan touched me, the "entity" released its grip on my throat. I gasped for air and sat on the edge of the bed. Dan began walking through the house, yelling once again and demanding that this "thing" leave our house immediately.

Neither of us slept the remainder of that night. In the morning we looked for the Sage we had stored away. The sage was lit and we smoked every nook and cranny of the house with it.

Needless to say we had enough. The invisible hands around my neck were the final straw. Everything up to this point had been academic and only a study of the Paranormal, but this had become very personal and possibly life threatening.

Many Television shows have developed due to the interest in the Paranormal. Primarily they feature those who investigate ghostly occurrences, in an attempt to acquire certain readings by use of conventional metering systems.

You have to ask yourself; "Where is all this leading?"

More importantly there is the question of the Spirit or Entity itself. What about them? What have these investigators done to help alleviate their problem? Have they offered them the help they need in moving on to their ultimate destination?

Unfortunately the general public isn't interested in the plight of the Entity, they are only interested in ambiguous read outs on a meter.

We attempted to coax Bill into the light many times. Although Bill expressed interest I don't believe he ever made it to the other side.

Many times we wondered if Bill was in fact who he said he was. There is nothing beyond the realm of possibilities when interacting with the Paranormal.

You cannot properly discern the non-physical world with physical instruments. Instruments tell us nothing of the complexity or the intent of the entity.

As a Burglar Alarm alerts you to the presence of someone, it tells you nothing of the intruder's character, nature, or place of origin.

I believe that many of those who we spoke to were on various "missions" with unknown objectives.

Some may have been Ghost as thought of in the traditional sense. Some may certainly have been lower Astral Entities. Perhaps some were mere interlopers.

The list is possibly endless, but to exclude anything at this point would be un-scientific. If we assume those Entities we encountered were but Ghost we would be limiting our thinking and in this Multi-verse, anything and everything you can possibly imagine is possible. Not only is it possible, but also if it can be imagined then it already exists!

We arrived at many conclusions during the course of our numerous conversations with the other side and the following are but a few of those things we discovered;

It is not possible to have a normal conversation with any of these entities.

They will never reveal to you the nature of their existence or where they come from.

Most of them are angry and use much profanity.

Some are benign types while others seem Demonic. Some may

be Tricksters as described in ancient folklores.

The ratio of male to female is probably around 75% male and 25% female.

Rarely have we conversed with children, other than our two visitors, though certainly children are taped often by other investigators and usually have a profound affect upon that investigator.

We have theorized that their responses to our questions are purposely ambiguous. We believe that the nature of their existence cannot be revealed to the living quite simply because they are not allowed to.

The veil of forgetfulness is in place upon our birth. This is purposeful and is used in conjunction with our free will. It is part of the plan. The Spirits must adhere to this law and may only reveal very little to us.

At the conclusion of every EVP session Dan would advise the Spirits to go to the light. He would gently tell them that their lives were no longer here on Earth, that they mustn't be afraid.

These words of direction and assurance appeared to have never worked since the same voices were present during the next and subsequent sessions.

There are those who have asked if speaking to the dead in this fashion only compounded our problems. To them I say no; the problems escalated prior to any EVP sessions and we believe they would have continued no matter what.

The EVP sessions did however give us a clearer understanding of what was happening in our home.

The Universe has many ways of speaking to you, and at times it does give you fair warning.

I was shopping one afternoon at a small Strip Mall not far from our home when an elderly woman approached me. She seemed to appear out of nowhere.

Her first words to me were that she thought I was very pretty. I thanked her and we chatted for a few moments.

Suddenly her demeanor became very serious.

"If you don't leave Tucson before its too late, it will have a hold of you, and it will destroy you!" She said.

Naturally I was a bit shocked. I thanked her for the advice and turned to enter my car. The thought occurred to me to offer her a ride home, but when I looked back toward her she was gone. I scanned the parking lot for her, but she had simply vanished.

The words she said to me were now repeating in my head on a daily basis.

The occurrence was so bizarre that I came to believe the old lady was not of flesh and blood, not in the normal sense that is. I believe that its possible that she was an inhabitant of an alternate realm, which at times interacts with ours in a desperate attempt to deliver a message or a warning.

As with the "Old Man" of my childhood who briefly pursued me with his own warning, he too had a message to deliver.

As the days dragged by I found that I was growing increasingly depressed, but certainly I wasn't alone in my depression. Studies indicated that those who lived in Tucson had an abnormally high incidence of depression. In fact most of our neighbors were on anti-depressants.

Was it simply a sign of the times, or was it Tucson?

I decided to seek additional advice and recalled listening to a radio show one evening where the program guest was a well-known Psychic by the name of Dr. Evelyn Paglini. Evelyn was the last in a one thousand year lineage of Strega Toscani Occult Practioneers. Evelyn is situated in Southern California and welcomes private readings. I am rarely impressed with Psychics, but Evelyn was a different story.

I called her by phone and booked a Reading with her.

"Get out of Arizona, it is not right for you or your Family. Your vibrations are way out of whack for this area and it will destroy you!" were her cryptic words. Evelyn made it very clear that we had inadvertently chosen the wrong area to move to.

I knew she was right of course. Evelyn advised us to move back to California as quickly as possible, or even another State, but we couldn't stay in Arizona as the entire State was vibrationally inhospitable to us.

We were out of sync in Arizona and this had become very obvious to us all.

It was also Tax time and no doubt this intensified my feelings of despair. I decided to put in a call to Peter our Accountant. I had numerous questions for him since Tax season was fast approaching and I wanted to put my mind at ease.

Peter also prepared my Fathers Taxes and had so for years.

"How is my Father" I asked Peter.

"He is fine Kathy, when is the last time you talked to him?" Peter asked.

"Its been a while Peter"

"Your Father was just diagnosed with Prostrate Cancer Kathy, maybe you should try calling him"

I said nothing to Dan for quite some time. I had to think about this. I couldn't stand another rejection from my Father. I had endured a lifetime of rejection from him.

A week or so had passed and I felt it was time to ask Dan his opinion. Dan's answer was pretty straightforward. Dan, not having been raised in any one faith was a very spiritual person, certainly more spiritual than religious, but his reply was right to the point.

"What would Jesus do in this case?" Dan asked.

Naturally he was right. I would put aside my feelings and my pride. That night I called my Father.

It had been almost eight years since we last spoke together.

Dad was very gracious on the phone. He told me that he was only waiting for an apology from me. He went on to say that he was my Father and I should show due respect.

The rebel in me wanted to jump through the phone at him, but I restrained myself and the rest of the conversation was very enjoyable.

I told him that I understood he had been diagnosed with Prostrate Cancer. He reassured me that his Doctor informed him that they believed it was diagnosed in time and his prognosis was very good.

He also informed me that he did not want to speak of it again.

My Father seemed to have changed, as his voice was very reassuring and calming, almost nurturing. We caught up on each other's lives and vowed to talk to each other again very soon. He also allowed my Mother to speak with me and for this I was most appreciative.

"Its got to be the Cancer, he's sensing his mortality" Dan said, as I placed the phone back on its cradle.

I was astonished. Was this my Father who I just spoke to?

Over the following weeks I spoke to my Parents on a regular basis. Plans were made for them to fly out and spend a few days at our home in Tucson.

When they arrived at the Airport we were there to meet them and took them directly back to our house as they appeared very tired from the trip. My Parents who were both now in their late seventies and I was somewhat shocked by how they appeared to have aged.

I re-introduced them to Dan and although Dan of course re-membered meeting them both, my Father claimed he didn't recall meeting Dan at all.

Dan felt he had a case of selective memory loss. On the two oc-casions where my Father met Dan he treated him in an extremely rude manner.

He made quite an everlasting impression upon Dan.

Amazingly, over the next few days both Dan and I found my Father to be very likeable. He was like the Father I never had and he and Dan got along fabulously together/

I felt as though my wounds were beginning to slowly heal dur-ing their brief stay with us. All I ever asked for was my Fathers ap-proval and love.

Perhaps he approves of me now I thought. Maybe he has recognized the fact that through our hard work and successes I was
able to purchase a beautiful home in an exclusive area of Tucson?
Maybe after seeing the gorgeous cars we drove he held me in
higher regard?

We were seated in the Dining room having Dinner one night
during his stay when he began shaking his head side to side. He
was in obvious disapproval of something.

"I got to be honest with you and tell you I don't care for your
house much," he said.

I looked toward Dan who was bringing the fork to his mouth
and then stopped abruptly.

"And what do you need with that fancy car in the garage, why
didn't you invest your money in something else?" he added.

I looked at Dan again and I could see he was doing his best to
ignore my Fathers remarks.

"Its not that the house is crappy, it's just not my style"

He continued eating.

"Dad, this is the style of the homes in this area, it's a Southwest-
ern home," I rebutted.

Having gotten his digs in he promptly changed the subject. The
remainder of the conversation centered on the merits of the area
he and my Mother now lived in.

My Father and Mother purchased a "cookie cutter" house in the
Dell Webb Sun City complex in Lincoln, California. It was a small
house with little maintenance. Actually the house was perfect for
two elderly people.

Before moving to Tucson we had contemplated looking at the Lincoln area that was situated just North of Sacramento. It was a quaint area near the Sierras Nevada Foothills. Lake Tahoe was only about an hour away. The area itself was rather flat and featureless but it had easy access to the recreation areas nearby.

My Father had engaged us in a somewhat flawed sales technique. I got the definite impression that he wanted us to move to that area, but why I didn't know.

My Parents departed Tucson the next day and returned to Lincoln. We settled back into what had become a humdrum existence. We had explored the area we lived in thoroughly and there was nothing left to explore. Life was becoming redundant.

I found myself becoming more and more depressed as the days slowly dragged by. Dan experienced a slight degree of depression but I believe what was more problematic for him were the unwelcome inhabitants of the house.

To make matters worse, our female Boxer Bonnie was diagnosed with Valley Fever.

Valley Fever is a spore that resides in soil. When the soil is disturbed, the spores may release and become airborne. Upon inhalation the spore spreads through the body of either the person or animal wreaking havoc with the organs. The contraction of this spore is often fatal.

Had we known of this problem we certainly never would have moved to Arizona. It was only through Holistic Animal therapy and Acupuncture that we were able to bring Bonnie back to health.

But the fix was only temporary.

I kept in touch with my Mother and Father and we talked almost on a daily basis. My Father suggested that we "get the hell out of there" and look for a home in his area.

I suggested this to Dan, and over the course of a few months the idea of a move back to California seemed more and more like a good idea.

There was nothing left for us in Arizona. After all we were Californians and despite the problems the State was experiencing, it was home.

Whether real or imagined, Tucson seemed to become increasingly unfriendly and we felt truly out of place.

In 2008 we made the decision to move. Dad was a Real Estate Broker and agreed to help in a search of homes. We agreed we would look for property in my Fathers area.

Dad suggested we come up for a few days and have a look around. We found a Dog Sitter and set out for a drive to Lincoln.

Our first few days there were wonderful and we fell in love with the Granite Bay area. Granite Bay is an upscale area near Folsom Ca. With beautifully manicured homes and Folsom Lake nearby its only draw back were the prices of the homes.

I was "shown" in the early 2000's that the Real Estate Market was going to recede into decline. The biggest mistake we made when we sold the San Mateo house was to invest every penny into our new Tucson home.

We too were conditioned to believe the false premise that the prices of homes would only go up in value. We just had to have that Tucson house and nothing would stand in the way.

In 2006 we discussed the idea of selling the house. We knew we should get out while there was still time, but we did not. Perhaps the move to Tucson in 2005 had taken a toll on us. The idea of moving again was almost incomprehensible to us. Besides, this was the house we were going to retire in, perhaps even dieing there.

We stayed with my Father during our search for our home. We were all getting along together quite well until our final night there.

After Dinner my Father and Dan engaged in what was at first a civilized political debate. Although the two were basically on the same page, it was something that Dan said concerning the present state of the economy and its relationship to President Bush's former policies that blew a mental gasket in my Fathers head.

My Fathers eyes literally glazed over as he rose from his chair. He began screaming; "Don't worry Dan you will be alright!"

He repeated this to Dan over and over again. His face turned bright red and it appeared he was losing his mind.

Dan rose from his chair also and began to make a slow retreat from the Living Room toward the bedroom we were staying in.

My Father pursued him to the bedroom repeating his chant over and over again. Dan pulled me inside the bedroom and slammed the door.

Dan told me during the drive home that he feared at that moment that my Father was going to physically attack him. He felt that my Father was simply crazy.

We had no further intercourse with my Father that night, and early the next morning we dressed and packed our things.

We were to leave that morning anyways. My Parents were up early and offered us Breakfast. Politely we refused and stated that we wanted to get an early start.

My Father put out his hand to say goodbye to Dan and they both shook hands. Dan quickly exited the house and walked to the car.

We began our drive back to Arizona and had only been gone for a couple of hours when my cell phone rang. It was my Father. The entire conversation centered on Dan and how I had made a big mistake by marrying him. I attempted to defend Dan but my Father would have nothing of it.

Once again he hung up on me.

It is my contention that my Father, always being one step ahead of everyone only fainted kindness during our visits and subsequent conversations. Unfortunately he was unable to continue the charade of being the kindly loving Father.

Dad always found a reason to despise his children's spouses.

And now it was Dan's turn. I don't believe it bothered Dan much however, as now Dan had a reason not to associate with him.

Over the coming months I continued to talk to my Father by phone almost daily. He rarely mentioned Dan's name and only did so when he wanted to get in another "jab" at him.

The Real Estate Market by then was in utter turmoil and finding a suitable home at a modest price was quite an endeavor.

In addition to buying a home we also considered a rental and actively sought one. Our major obstacle with a rental centered on the fact they we had three dogs. The majority of Landlords and especially those in your higher end rentals will not allow pets.

Another big problem as we were to discover was the fact that many of the rental homes were nearing foreclosure or were in some other state of financial distress.

We decided to forget a rental and buy.

At the same time we had also placed the Tucson house up for sale, but the market in Tucson was also in disarray. There were many lookers but no offers.

My Father grew tired of searching for property. "Stay in Tucson" was just one of his utterances after almost a year of looking.

I believe he was simply growing plain old tired. Tests had shown that the Cancer had spread from his Prostrate to his bones. He was indeed slowing down.

And then one morning our Agent in California called and said she had found the perfect home for us. It was in Roseville and she thought it was just what we were looking for, and the price was right.

Pictures of the property were sent via e-mail and within a few days we made the decision to buy. Within a month our loan was approved through the Bank and all loose ends were tied up.

We would be moving in July. The Tucson house would remain on the market and we would simply leave the sale in the hands of our Agent in Tucson.

We hired a moving Company and began packing immediately.

I can't begin to tell you how happy I was. I knew that if we stayed in this house it would kill one of us. I told Dan this numerous times. I believe it would be the demise of one of us.

Unfortunately, I wasn't far off.

It was a Monday morning, and the following day the Moving Company was slated to arrive.

I was taking my daily tour of our front yard area when I discovered a really disturbing site. Our property was covered in various Desert Plants, Saguaros, Cholas, and many large Barrel Cacti. It was on one of the Barrel Cactus not far from our front door where a large bird had apparently impaled himself. The Bird obviously flew directly into the Barrel Cactus, which was only about three feet tall, and harpooned himself on two or three of the large thorns that protruded from it. It was frozen in a Death pose with its head tilted toward the sky, with wings outstretched and his chest pierced.

I stepped away and took a deep breath. Running back to the house I called for Dan to come outside. Dan reluctantly stopped his packing and walked outside shaking his head as if to say "what is it now?" I was always finding snakes, spiders, or scorpions and then calling for Dan hysterically.

"Oh my God" was Dan's as he took a close look at this bizarre scene.

"How in the world could this happen? He flew directly into the Cactus. Maybe he committed suicide? Dan remarked as he gazed upon this truly unusual spectacle.

It wasn't until weeks later that Dan told me what he really

thought as he gazed upon the Bird.

Dan told me that upon seeing the Bird it immediately dawned on him that it was a sign. This was a sign of impending Death. A warning to us, given only two days before leaving Arizona. Dan told me that he did not want to say anything then because he did not want to upset or scare me.

In cultures of indigenous people throughout the world, Birds or often described as harbingers of things to come.

Dan told me once of a friend of his Mothers who was married and lived on the third floor of an apartment building. Her friend noticed that for three days in a row, a little sparrow would land on the window ledge in her bedroom and peck at the window. He would leave then return minutes later and continue his pecking. This odd behavior by the Sparrow was observed over a three-day period. On the fourth day her husband was lying on the bed in this room and suffered a sudden and lethal heart attack. The arriving medical crew pronounced him dead in that room. His Mothers friend knew beyond a doubt that the Sparrow was announcing his death. The Sparrow never returned after that day.

Certainly it's possible that birds fly into Cactus in the Desert and impale themselves accidentally. But I for one do not believe in coincidences.

The drive back to California was a long one, but I couldn't care less, when we drove across that California line, all I could do was breathe a sigh of relief. We made it back and we were all in good health.

We arrived at our new house and began unpacking what we

brought with us in the cars and a small trailer.

It was July and very hot. Two days later the Moving Company arrived with all of our household goods and needless to say the following days were very busy in getting our new home together.

The following Saturday we too a breather and really was our first chance to sit down and enjoy our new surroundings. Bonnie, our Boxer was in the backyard and we noticed that she was acting very strangely.

Later that night, Bonnie began throwing up. The throwing up continued to the point that we were forced to bring her down to the only Veterinarian Office open twenty four hours.

After viewing the x-rays the Doctor informed us that Bonnie had an enlargement in her intestines. She recommended immediate surgery.

We were stunned. But we also decided that before surgery we would get a second opinion.

We took Bonnie home that night and the next day we found a Vet nearby who could examine her Sunday morning.

His opinion was the same, he recommended immediate surgery. We gave the go ahead and Bonnie went in for surgery. A couple of hours passed and the Vet called us at home. The Vet had removed one and a half feet of "bad" intestine. He told us he had never seen anything like it before.

We explained to him that Bonnie had contracted Valley Fever three years ago. Valley Fever is a spore that resides naturally in the soil. When dislodged from the soil and inhaled it begins attacking the organs of the body. Not only animals die from this, our Bank

Manager contracted it, and died within months. Our neighbor's son contracted it when they began building a shopping center nearby. It is rampant in the Southern Arizona area. Had we known this before hand we would never have moved to Arizona. Bonnie through natural remedies and acupuncture, along with a very expensive medicine through the Vet had made a recovery from it.

Bonnie was transferred to another Vet Hospital for "intensive care" but her condition rapidly deteriorated. We were informed she also had bone cancer. They believed the cancer might have also been a direct result of the Valley Fever. Bonnie was in great pain as she lay on the small mat provider her within the "recovery" cage. Her eyes darted back and forth indicating Neurological damage.

We made the decision to put her to sleep.

That day we lost our "Daughter". Bonnie was an incredibly beautiful Boxer and outwardly appeared to be in the best of health, but the Valley Fever ate her insides up. We were actually lucky that she lived as long as she did.

We were devastated and still haven't gotten over her loss.

The "warning" of the impaled Bird in our front yard proved true!

Tucson had taken one of us, as sure as if it had taken Dan or myself.

I think Dan would have preferred that it taken him instead, and not Bonnie.

Unfortunately I was right again. I wish I had been completely wrong when I warned that one of us would die because of Tucson.

CHAPTER FOURTEEN

California

W e were now living only minutes from my Father and Mother and I visited quite often. Of course Dan was not allowed over, nor was I allowed to even mention his name.

My Fathers health continued to do well, his PSA was way down and all other tests showed promising results.

With the exception of the loss of Bonnie and the emptiness we felt without her, life was good.

We enjoyed seeing "green" once again. Tree lined streets, fresh air replenished by the "Delta Breezes" which supplied the valley with tons of fresh air from the ocean.

Yes, we were home again, and I relished every moment.

The following weeks encompassed a settling in period. We explored new towns and took long drives through the forest watching in stunned silence at the beauty in which He created.

We decided on adopting another Boxer and we located a Breeder in Lake Tahoe. The Bitch had seven pups but none were old enough to bring home yet. Dan picked a little female from the litter and we gave the Breeder a down payment. We would pick

Abbey up on Dan's birthday in August. She was a beautiful little female and we couldn't wait to bring her home.

In November my Father called and told me that the latest test results had come back high.

My Father was of the opinion that he wasn't sick at all.

"Kathy, both you and I know that there is nothing whatsoever wrong with me!"

With Thanksgiving approaching I was saddled a very large problem. I wanted the entire Family for Dinner, but of course my Father was still refusing to talk with Dan.

I decided to call my Father.

"I will not have Dinner in the same house as that Bloody Asshole!" he screamed.

I was forced to pull the phone from my ear. This man isn't sick I thought. Perhaps my Brother Steve was right when he told me months earlier that the apparent change in my Fathers demeanor was nothing more than a ploy. Steve felt my Father was up to something. I scoffed at the idea and told him the change was genuine. I attributed the sudden turn around to illness and an awakening to his mortality.

Looking back I must admit that Steve was right.

I really began to question the medical diagnosis. Maybe my Father was right, maybe he wasn't sick at all.

Dan wasn't the only one my Father had on the exclusion list. Robs wife Barbara, and Cindy's husband Carlos made the list also.

And there were others!

I couldn't take my Fathers yelling any longer and I began

screaming back at him. I informed him that if Dan wasn't allowed then neither was he, and I hung up.

"Did that come out of me?" I thought as I let go of the phone.

We had a Family Thanksgiving without my Father or Mother that year.

Christmas came and went too with no word from my Father or my Mother.

In early January of 2010 I received a call from my Brother Rob. Rob told me he had just spoken to Dad and he wasn't doing very well. Dad's pride wouldn't allow him to call me, but he asked Rob to please have me call him.

I called my Father right away. There was no mention of our previous argument during the conversation. My Fathers voice sounded weak and he was somewhat disoriented.

He needed my help.

I hung up and drove straight to his house. Mom answered the door. Looking straight into my eyes she appeared puzzled.

"Yes?" she uttered.

"Mom it's me, Kathy" I said.

My Mother seemed to snap out of a stupor. She stood aside and motioned to me to come in.

It was obvious my Mothers Dementia had grown worse since I saw her last.

My Father was lying in bed and he appeared to have lost an enormous amount of weight. According to my Mother he had become incontinent and the house smelled strongly of human waste.

Dad explained that the cancer had spread to his bones and the

Doctor placed him on a regimen of drips in order to strengthen his bones. He further explained that he took a turn for the worse immediately after treatment began.

During the following weeks I provided care to my Father on a daily basis. My Mothers Dementia was escalating and she was barely capable of providing for herself, let alone tending to my Fathers needs.

Dad was spending most of his time in bed. Well-balanced meals were out of the question and he refused to eat anything that I cooked for him instead, craving only sweets and fast foods.

It wasn't long before I found myself beginning to tire. I didn't feel good. I found it incredibly draining. I was advised by numerous people who told of similar incidents of relatives who provided care to the dieing. They told of caregivers who themselves became sick, and of some who succumbed to the experience.

I was beginning to understand the truth of their warnings.

My marriage was beginning to suffer also. I was rarely home and it was only for a late dinner then falling into bed from complete emotional and physical exhaustion.

Dan was very accommodating and never complained. Each night he had my Dinner ready and he was filled with words of encouragement and praise for what I was doing.

I missed not having a life.

My Mother spent her days sitting on the couch starring at the Television. Now and then she would turn her gaze from the Television to say hello to unseen guest who she would announce by name as they entered the room. She saw children also, and had conversations with them. From moment to moment her reality changed. I would sit with her and have perfectly lucid conversations and in the next moment she wouldn't know who I was.

My Father had become thoroughly emaciated, but you never would have known this judging by the vitality of his voice. He was constantly calling for me making demand after demand coupled with a continuous barrage of insults.

Each day became increasingly dark and depressing for me.

In the back of my mind I knew beyond a doubt that if I were in their position and I needed their help they would not be there for me. This idea of course was not conjecture on my part. When I was dieing and needed help they completely abandoned me. They called each and every relative telling them that my illness was "all in her head". They even advised my Aunt to stop all visits and "Let her die!"

Despite this I was determined to help them. It went beyond obligation. As long as I was physically able I would do all that I could.

Admittedly I was bitter. Dan understood the feelings and resentment that I harbored within. He counseled that this was a learning process for my Parents. I was given a set of circumstances where I could demonstrate to them first hand what love truly meant. It would have a profound affect upon their higher selves despite their initial and apparent unappreciative reaction.

He was right of course.

As my Mothers apparent delusions seemed to be on the increase, so too my Father began experiencing his own visions.

As I lay on his bed massaging his right hand he looked up and pointed toward the ceiling. He appeared to be in communication with some one or something as he nodded his head up and down in an apparent acknowledgement. This lasted for maybe a minute then abruptly ended. He seemed drained. I asked him what he saw. He told me they were appearing to him but he didn't know who they were. He went on to say that they told him everything was going to be all right!

It was at that moment that I knew there was no coming back for my Father. He was dieing. It was just a matter of time. There would be no recovery.

As my Father grew physically weaker my Mothers delusions grew stronger.

She was sleeping very little now and spending most of the night keeping my Father awake.

I feared that one night she would depart the house and simply disappear.

We had to take some sort of additional action. I talked with Cynthia and together we agreed to research the feasibility of employing a full time Caregiver.

After much research we decided against hiring a live in Caregiver. We needed an alternative and we began to look at an Assisted Living center.

A week later we located a Center not far from my Parents home. The Center had a good reputation and the costs were reasonable.

My Father actually welcomed the move. I can only assume that he felt it would be a more secure environment for both he and my Mother. I do not believe my Mother fully understood that she would be moving from her home, but as long as she remained with Dad we all assumed she would fair well.

My Mother and Father quickly settled into their new surroundings. Their apartment was quite nice actually and afforded them a wonderful view of the surrounding mountains. It included all amenities except a kitchen. All meals were prepared downstairs by the cooks and the residents had their choice of eating in the Dining room or taking their meals in their rooms.

The Staff appeared competent and extremely gracious. Naturally my Father did not adhere to this view. It wasn't long before he began to verbally abuse the staff with the most vile language imaginable. Naturally the staff experienced personalities like my Fathers in the pass and they all seemed to take his abuse in stride.

But now, and much to the utter surprise of my Father he too would fall victim to verbal abuse and from the person who he never would have suspected!

After 61 years of marriage, my Mother had finally had enough. The years of resentment that boiled just below the surface but was always restrained would now surface in all its fury.

The verbal retribution began one morning as though some unseen hand had flipped a switch in my Mothers mind and she continued non-stop through the night. The only respite my Father experienced was when she slept. Upon awakening my Mother wasted no time in lashing out at him once again. After but a few days my Father begged me to "get rid of her". He couldn't take it any longer. One of them had to go and my Father cared not who it was.

He now referred to her as "that Bitch"

Admittedly we all chuckled at this. After all we are only human. It was retribution for the decades of abuse and domination she endured. Certainly the timing was a little late in coming. In a way we were proud of Mom for finally speaking up and asserting herself.

The visions continued to persist for my Father. I witnessed his apparent conversations with the steady stream of invisible visitors to his room. The staff I talked said they see this a lot in terminal patients. They felt it was nothing more than delusions.

I of course knew better!

He was taking little "trips" also. He related how he would visit mysterious lands and then suddenly he was back in his bed. He couldn't understand what was happening.

But he did know that he wanted his companion of 61 years out of his hair and out of his life. My Mother was driving him crazy!

Eight weeks into my Parents stay at the center there was an incident with my Father involving another apparent visitation. As I sat on my Mothers bed I could see that my Fathers attention was focused on the front door leading to the hallway. His arm was outstretched as though he was pointing. I looked to my right and toward the door and standing only feet away was an outline of a person. Initially I thought one of the staff had entered the room unannounced.

This form stood there motionless. I struggled to ask what he wanted, but I was unable to get out any words.

He was old and gaunt and I was even able to see the deep lines in his face. With a large nose and thin un-moving lips he appeared grizzled and un-shaven.

He wore a large brimmed hat and a dark coat that reached to the floor.

I let out a loud gasp. "Who the hell are you?" I screamed.

With those words the old man took two steps backwards and disappeared.

My gaze turned to my Father as I could see that the hand he had outstretched a moment before was now being lowered. His head turned to the left as it sunk back into the pillow.

My Mother was completely unaware of what had just occurred.

I rushed to my Fathers side only to find they had fallen back to sleep.

Memories began rushing back into my psyche.

Remembrances of the Old Man who chased me during my youth poured back into my mind. I have seen this Specter many times in the past.

But this time the Old Man was focused on my Father and not me!

Badly shaken, I was barely able to negotiate the twenty-minute drive home. Once again I was witness to this strange presence, only this time I fully understood the message his presence brought.

As the days passed, my Father grew increasingly weak. He was barely able to speak and complained constantly of pain in his groin area. A staff member took me aside and suggested I take him into the hospital. I concurred with this and immediately called Dads Doctor.

The following day Dad was taken via Ambulance to the Emergency Room. The Doctor ordered a Transfusion and additional tests.

The Doctor was very solemn when he took me aside that afternoon.

"Kathy, I suggest you take your Father out of Assisted Living and place him in Skilled Nursing. Your Fathers condition is deteriorating quickly and his Kidney disease has entered Stage Four"

"What Kidney disease, no one ever told me he has Kidney Disease," I gasped.

"Your Father has had Kidney disease for quite some time now. I am sorry he never informed you of this, but now you need to take my advice and find a skilled Nursing Facility for him"

I informed Cindy of the diagnosis and the recommendation that Dad be placed in a Skilled Facility.

Placing my Father in a Skilled Nursing facility would be fairly easy, but what about my Mother, what would we do with her?

Cindy insisted that Dad and Mom come live with her and Carlos. I didn't argue with the offer. I was physically and emotionally exhausted from the last few months and thought it was an excellent idea.

Father was taken back to the Assisted Nursing complex that night after receiving a Transfusion at the Hospital. The Transfusion appeared to have worked wonders for him.

I arrived at the Facility the next day. I had an offer I wanted to run by my Father.

I explained to my Father that instead of being placed in a Skilled Nursing Facility as recommended by the Doctor, Cindy and Carlos would bring him into their home where they could provide for all his needs.

My Father slowly turned his head and said; "I would never move into that damn house with Carlos, he's a total Asshole!"

To Dad Carlos was simply another spouse, and spouses were all held in the lowest regard.

"Okay" I said. "Then would you consider moving in with Dan and I?"

"Kathy, stop being ridiculous, Dan is a bigger Asshole than Carlos"

I should have known better, but I had to try.

I explained to Dad that his only other alternative was another Nursing Facility.

"Then that's where I will go" was his stubborn response.

I informed Cindy of Dads refusal to move in with one of us. Cindy was fine with the idea of Dad going to a Nursing Facility. She decided that she would take Mom to live with her once Dad was moved.

We decided Dad would be moved to a Facility in the Sacramento and we located one in the Citrus Heights area.

Two days later we moved Dad into the new Facility.

As the attendants were moving Dad from his room and into the waiting transport Mom approached him in an attempt to say goodbye.

"Get her the hell away from me!" he yelled.

These were the final words my Father would ever say to my Mother.

It would also be the last time the two would ever be together.

CHAPTER FIFTEEN

Revelations

It was recommended that I wait a day or two before visiting my Father in his new surroundings. There is a settling in period that Patients must go through and early visits by relatives and friends are considered disruptive to the Patient in their new environment.

But I had little time to wait, as I knew in my heart that my Father would be taken at any time.

I waited a full day and then on the second day I drove to the Skilled Nursing complex.

It was an older Brick building nestled in a middle class neighborhood. The complex itself was horseshoe shaped with long dark hallways. The Staff was friendly and they directed me to my Fathers room.

Each room contained three beds. Each bed had an accompanying nightstand. There was nothing else in the room.

My Father had two roommates. Both were elderly men and both were terminal with Cancer. As I entered the room I noticed that my Fathers roommates were both asleep as was my Father.

"What a drab and depressing environment" I thought.

My Father should be with family I thought, but his current predicament was of his own choosing. Certainly Dan would have welcomed him into our house during these final days and even suggested to me that I present the idea to my Father.

It was no time to harbor a grudge, but my Father was a very stubborn man.

I sat at the foot of my Fathers bed and looked to his face and chest for signs of life. Father must have sensed my presence slowly opening his eyes. Reaching out to me we clutched each others hands. I told him I loved him.

"I love you too Kathy, I hope you know I have always loved you. You have always been my favorite, you know that don't you?"

Were these loving words actually coming from my Father? I wondered.

We spent the rest of the day reminiscing old times and exclaiming just how much we meant to each other.

Those were the most joyous moments I have ever spent with my Father.

It was almost Dinnertime and I told Dad that I would be back the following day.

I bent over to kiss him goodnight when he once again grabbed my hand.

"Kathy you have to get me out of here, if you don't get me out of here I'm going to die" he said pleading to me.

I repeated my offer to bring him my home to live. He agreed to the suggestion, but only on one condition; Dan would have to move out.

"I don't think that's going to happen Dad, but Dan said he would be happy to have you come stay with us".

"Kathy, Kathy, Kathy, you and I both know that will never happen" With that he motioned for me to go by the wave of his hand.

I turned and left the room. As I walking down that dark and depressing hallway I began to cry. By the time I reached the front door I was crying so badly I could barely locate my car in the lot.

I cried all the way home and was a basket case by the time I walked into the house.

I visited my Father daily and our talks became more in depth. He continued to greet visitors who were unseen to me and anyone else. His conversations with them consisted of no more than a few words of acknowledgement. Physically and mentally he appeared to me to be improving.

And then during one visit my Father; the perennial disbeliever in anything other than current conventional thought began asking me questions about my Near Death Experience. I remember telling him of this many years before, but the subject was never brought up again as he dismissed the idea outright.

My Father considered himself a good Catholic though he rarely attended Church.

I spent many hours with my Father over the next couple of days explaining to him in detail what the other side looks like. Because of the stage of life he was now in he was genuinely interested in everything I had to say.

It was a funny thing, but in retrospect while in his presence I remembered only the good moments spent with him, not the negative. I was somewhat confused as I later pondered this and it occurred to me that those unpleasant and sometimes brutal moments were not important. What was important were the positive and nurturing encounters my Father and I experienced together. It was through these encounters that growth occurred.

I suppose he wanted to believe everything I told him during these final talks. It was only a matter of time before he would fully realize the truth of my words.

We shall all discover the truth, some sooner and some a little later.

Miraculously my Father was now becoming a believer. But he wanted to know more.

He called me a "witch" in my youth and now he was telling me that he always believed that I had a gift, but he also explained that my "gift" conflicted with his religious up bringing. In retrospect perhaps he did believe it all along.

I believe he was at a loss as to what to believe, but he wanted to know more. He wanted to know how accurate I was. In the end he wanted proof.

I explained to him that I have been giving people readings for as far back as I can remember. Sometimes if I was off somewhat on what I saw it was only because of the free will that we are given on this plane of existence. The future is not always fixed and it can vary taking many courses, but sometimes certain things are in fact fixed and cannot be changed.

As he starred at the ceiling he said; "I want you to give me a reading Kathy!"

Needless to say I was shocked.

"I want to know if all of you will be alright. I want to make sure Ira will be okay. I want to know what is in store for the world," he said softly. There was much worry in his voice and in his expression.

Taking his hand once again I looked into his eyes.

"Dad I will explain it all to you. If you believe me then you will understand why you are here and what the World has in store for all of us. Do you trust me to tell you the truth?" I asked.

"I trust you Kathy, now tell me the truth. I want to know it all. I don't care about what happens fifty years from now I wont be here then, nobody will, tell me what will happen for the next ten years. We both know I will make it another ten years. I don't want to know any more than that, now tell me"

"Alright Dad I will tell you what is in store for all of us. I must warn that you may not like what you hear"

I took a deep breath and slowly released it. I turned away from my Father and focused my attention through the nearby window. I said a prayer and asked to be shown what I was shown before but not have seen since.

With this warning I began.

"The next ten years will not be good. The majority of those measures put into place to protect us from this Boogie Man who they refer to as Terrorist is nothing more than a rouse for the powers that be to control us.

The "shadow controllers" understand that the entire economic system of the world is collapsing. It was designed to collapse.

These control systems have been introduced incrementally and very quietly and the majority of the people believe it's for their own good. It is not!

Americans have become a self-absorbed ignorant people who know nothing of history and are fated to repeat what many Countries have endured in the past. It is through this lack of knowledge and awareness that the greatest pilferage of wealth in the history of mankind is taking place. I am sad to tell you that we have seen nothing yet.

What the world braces for in 2012 or, more specifically December 21st, 2012 when the Mayan Calendar ends is nothing more than an awakening, an epiphany by the majority of people of this planet who up to this point have been in a controlled slumber.

The Social Engineers or rather the ruling elite loses their grip on the "reality" they created for their subjects during this coming time.

But the sleeping giant begins to rouse during this time. I see the awakening beginning to happen by the summer of 2011. But even before this time the people will experience a stir of consciousness. This change of attitude and subservience toward the authoritarian ruling class will begin with mass protest and Civil Disobedience. The protest will progress from peaceful to violent as Austerity measures are put into place. The American people who grew accustomed to living an opulent and lavish life style now find that American Dream has crashed and burned. Those who said it couldn't happen here will be the ones who did not prepare for these times. They are the ones who didn't take history seriously.

This is the time that the Revolution or Civil Wars will begin. The old saying that we are only three meals away from a Revolution is a truism and we will certainly realize this in the latter part of 2011. This is also the time when Marital Law begins in earnest. The infrastructure for this Marital Law has already been put into place by the powers that be for this time because their highly priced Think Tanks and computer models told them of this.

I see the economy continuing to falter and will not bottom until around 2015. By then the United States we have all known will be but a shell of its former self. The world will be convinced that America has completely imploded, but they will be incorrect in this assumption.

The United States will not be the only country to suffer through this. The entire World is plunged into Depression and extreme Austerity. The United States in terms of violence is hit the hardest. Perhaps this is due to the number of firearms in the country. The people have a means of active revolt. The majority of other countries do not.

The American people wake up to the fact this country has been completely de-industrialized and it was not by mistake or miscalculation on the part of our leaders.

What the powers that be have failed to consider is that a mass resistance by a people subjugated under a Police State or Military occupation almost always succeeds as it has in Iraq and Afghanistan. The Russians and many empires before them went down in defeat due to the indeterminable will of the people.

The Elite believe that somehow this will end differently for them, but they will have mis-calculated.

I see the youth of our country and many other countries as not only the heroes of freedom and righteousness, but they will be the survivors quite literally of the cleansing that is about to occur. There will be a large percentage of those alive now who will not make it through the coming years.

Starvation and pestilence will cull the population worldwide. The in fighting too will have a profound affect on the population numbers. Competing interest among the people not just the Government will be a cause for much of the bloodshed.

There will come a heightening of Telepathic powers. These powers will be most evident in the youngest among us. Those who will be our future leaders will combine their Telepathic abilities with a new generation of electronics. With this leap in technology there will be a leap in the spiritual nature of man. No longer will the young spend endless hours with trendy electronics as they waste their precious time with frivolous and meaningless entertainment.

The very nature and understanding that man will possess will look nothing like that of which we see around us today. It will be a true awakening of the soul, but this will not happen for at least another decade.

I liken the awakening to a Near Death Experience. This is how profound it will be. It will be a world wide and complete awakening to the true nature of self.

The shackles of the New World Order controllers will be thrown off.

There will be no WWIII during this time and that which we call Armageddon will not come to fruition during the next decade. But the destruction that will occur will be equal to or greater than that of a Nuclear War.

All of this is necessary. This is a cleansing and the "die off" occurs during any cleansing.

What is left of civilization will be completely different than what it looks like today. I do not see the United States breaking up into regions. But I do see certain States banning together to fight the common enemy of Freedom.

We will retain our Constitution, but there will be a Constitutional Convention whereby measures and wording within the Constitution will be re-affirmed and constructed so that there is no misinterpretation of its intent. Those who intend to destroy the Constitution because of its ambiguous language or unclear intent will never again be able to do so.

Government will be much smaller as it was intended to be. The people will once again embrace God as the divine creator. People will once again truly communicate with each other rather than using electronics as an intermediary.

The Family will once again become the most important thing.

As with the physical body when you cleanse it, all parts are cleansed.

We are all one and we are one with the Universe. Since this is true the changes will be symptomatic and evident on all levels and affect all things that we know.

There will be Earthquakes and extreme weather. There will be a changing quite literally of the lands. Coastlines will be changed; the interiors of countries will be changed as in the blink of an eye.

And the people who are now fully awake will turn upon those who have enslaved them. These controllers who thought they were safe in their computer models will be completely surprised and over run by a people who can no longer be restrained through mass hypnosis and lies.

Justice will be swift and there will be no traditional trials for these people as they are sought out and dealt with in quick fashion. No bunkers in the Midwest, no hidden and guarded Chalets in the Alps and no remote Islands in the Pacific will conceal them from the wrath of a newly awakened people.

And so the chains will be broken, but this will come at a very heavy price.

When the history books are re-written many will be shocked concerning how we were lied to on so many subjects. The history and nature of man has been hidden from us for many hundreds of years. The profoundness, the utter scope and complexity of the lies we have been systematically taught will astound the newer generations, so much so in fact that new measures will be put into place so that it may never happen again.

The mass deception of mankind will never again be repeated.

There are many who I refer to as having "dust in their eyes". By this I reference those who continue to believe in the popular paradigms because the truth would be too much for them to bear. These people find safety in the little mental box that was created for them preferring this because it is comfortable.

Cognitive dissonance by the majority of people will be overcome and the awakening will occur.

There is nothing new under the sun and what is occurring now has happened many times in our past dating back millions of years.

But even with safeguards in place, there will be those in the future who once again conspire to rule the world.

Countless times has our species rose to this level of technology and beyond when through the sickness of mans spirit we have fallen back into the Dark Ages only to emerge once again as an advanced Society, only to fall again. The cycle has been almost endless.

I turned and looked at my Father. His mouth was wide open as he starred in obvious shock and disbelief.

"Kathy, do you actually believe this stuff you are saying? This is America Kathy, we will never fall like that"

"Dad you wanted the truth and this is what I was shown. I have never really looked at it before because to tell you the truth I didn't want to look at it. All of which I spoke will come to pass. But we will be all right. Mom will be al-right. We will all come through this together"

I found it impossible to tell him that he wouldn't be there when this all happened.

"Okay, okay, that's enough for today. Now go home to your Husband, I will see you tomorrow maybe and by the way Kathy, I love you"

I kissed my Father goodbye and watched as he quickly drifted off to sleep.

As I walked the hallway toward the exit I had a profound sense of dread or perhaps a deep feeling of finality. I did not want to examine the feeling I was now experiencing. By the time I reached my car the emotions poured from deep within my soul. I sat in the car unable to start it for quite some time crying almost hysterically. I am not sure exactly how long I was in this state before I was able to start the engine and begin my drive home.

Reaching home I felt completely drained, but at the same time I felt clarity and a reconciliation, which I find difficult to put into words.

I awoke the next morning and for the first time in months I once again felt like the old me. For the first time in months I had my energy back. The depression that had gained momentum over the last few months seemed gone.

I dressed, poured myself a cup of coffee and picked up the phone. I never called Skilled Nursing before, but on this day I felt compelled to do so. As the phone rang an overwhelming "knowing" coursed through my body.

My Father was dead and I knew he was dead. I needed confirmation.

Moments later one of the Nurses picked up the phone. "How is my Father doing this morning?" I inquired.

The Nurse put me on hold and promised to check on him and get back.

Ten or more minutes passed and the Nurse hadn't returned. Thinking I had been disconnected I hung up and called back. This time the phone continued to ring and no one answered. I hung up once again and quickly called back.

The phone was answered this time. "Is this Kathy Baker?" she said. I told her it was. "I'm sorry Ms. Baker but your Father Leonard has just passed!"

I thanked her and told her I would be down immediately. She informed me that they kept the deceased in their rooms no more than two hours for family viewing before they move them to another area.

I called my Sister Cindy and my Brother Rob. I had hoped that Cindy would agree to bring my Mother up, but Cindy refused to do so stating that it would be too upsetting for her now. Rob told me that he could be there but it would impossible to make it from San Francisco to the Nursing home in only two hours.

It understood that it didn't really matter. My Father was no longer here because he was off on an incredible adventure.

I called Kim and Katrina. Together the three of us drove to the Center. There were no tears during that drive. In fact I felt an incredible release. The release wasn't for myself, but for my Father. He was now free.

Often times the dieing will pick the time that they pass. They will often pass at a time when Family members are not present sparing those members grief and anguish. This apparently is how my Father chose to leave, with as little fanfare as possible. Where others will choose their Death at home surrounded by loved ones, some will not.

We were quickly ushered into my Fathers room. His two roommates were unaware of his Death, as they both lay asleep in their beds. The Nurses had tidied up my Father and re-made his bed with tightly tucked corners and crisp folds at his chest.

He appeared almost angelic in his Death pose. Still laying on his back with eyes closed and lips pursed he was a shadow of his former self. Knowing he was dead I nevertheless searched for any signs of life, but he was still, frozen in his final moments.

I stood starring for quite sometime. Somehow the reality of his death had not sunken completely in.

Many thoughts ran through my mind during those moments.

How blessed I feel that if had the opportunity to sit with my Father during his most intimate of moments while dieing and to share our experiences in life both joyous and sad. I cannot help but to feel he experienced more sadness than joy and yet it was these lessons that he chose for himself.

When we are self centered love is difficult to find. And so it was with my Father. Friends and Family members ask me why I chose to come back to my Father. My answer to this was a very simple one; I went back because I loved him, I loved him unconditionally.

By the mere demonstration and by the expression of my unrequited love, my Father found that love was possible. He discovered that love really does exist outside of himself. He learned that love is something that doesn't belong just to him, but it must be shared and it must be demonstrated. Love is the strongest power in the Universe and no one can resist its overwhelming presence, not even my Father.

I recalled a conversation Dad and I had a few days prior where my Father described in perfect detail his encounter with what he described as an Angel. The Angel assisted him in an abbreviated life review. The Angel told my Father that everything my Father had done was now etched in the record book. The Angel told him that the most important thing on the Earthly plane besides love, and love of self was free will and how we use our free will. The Angel explained to him that it was a part of Gods plan.

I understood that nothing created by man is perfect. Only the Great Spirit is perfect in all that "He" does. When we are open to God and ready to learn of unconditional love He will at that point send into our lives, or place at an early age those in our lives whom we can practice unconditional love with. I have not been perfect at it this nor has my Father. Certainly he fell leagues short of that ideal because with him the idea of love was completely conditional. My Father was unable to forgive himself first. He was unable to unconditionally forgive and love himself therefore it was impossible for him to forgive and love others to the extent that he should have. It must first be found within.

I fully understand now that what little love my Father demonstrated for me was in direct relationship to his spiritual growth at this stage of his evolution. I wanted more of his love, but for now it was enough. He and I will be together again as our lives will cross many times in the future. Of this I am certain.

My Father is now in a room nearby, but not far from here. What binds us is our love for each other. Unconditional love is a process, an ideal that we shall all attain one day; of this I am sure.

CPSIA information can be obtained at www.ICGtesting.com
Printed in the USA
270541BV00001B/14/P